MANAGING THE MALAYSIAN ECONOMY

Challenges & Prospects

RAMON V. NAVARATNAM

MANAGING THE MALAYSIAN ECONOMY

Challenges & Prospects

Pelanduk
Publications

Published by
Pelanduk Publications (M) Sdn. Bhd.,
(113307-W)
24 Jalan 20/16A, 46300 Petaling Jaya,
Selangor Darul Ehsan, Malaysia.

Address all correspondence to
Pelanduk Publications (M) Sdn. Bhd.,
P.O. Box 8265, 46785 Kelana Jaya,
Selangor Darul Ehsan, Malaysia.

Cover photograph © Patrick Yap/Picture Library.
*Picture on cover depicts the Kuala Lumpur City skyline by night,
dominated by the Kuala Lumpur City Centre (KLCC) Twin Towers,
the world's tallest building.*

Perpustakaan Negara Malaysia   Cataloguing-in-Publication Data

Navaratnam, Ramon V.
    Managing the Malaysian economy:
    challenges and prospects / Ramon V. Navaratnam.
    ISBN 967-978-581-5
    1. Economic forecasting—Malaysia. 2. Malaysia—Economic
    policy. 3. Civil service—Malaysia. 4. Malaysia—Social conditions.
    5. Malaysia—Foreign relations. I. Title.
    338.9595

Printed in Malaysia by
Academe Art & Printing Services Sdn. Bhd.

For my dear late father,
Mr K.R. Navaratnam,
who served the Government
with dedication,
and my devoted mother,
Mrs Ruth Navaratnam,
who sacrificed much so that
I may do well in life.

And also for my
devoted wife, Samala,
and our three fine sons,
Ravi, Indran and Dharmen,
and our lovely
daughter-in-law, Premila,
who I hope will carry on
the tradition of positive and
constructive criticism
as Malaysian nationalists.
For it is our children's
generation who will inherit
and build upon all that
we have striven to achieve
since Independence
so as to realise the noble
goals of Vision 2020.

PREFACE

THE purpose of this book is to stimulate public discussion of Malaysia's major socio-economic issues—its challenges and prospects.

I thought it might be useful to express my views, and reflect on those of others, on the economic growth and development of Malaysia. We read so much that comes from government sources that we run the risk of being conditioned by only one major source of analysis and assessment of current trends. This may not be healthy as we need to encourage more critical and constructive thought on the issues of the day, to keep on track in achieving Vision 2020.

I am neither political nor ideological. I would consider myself a moderate, independent and pragmatic Malaysian nationalist, who is trying to contribute towards developing a Malaysian consciousness or *Bangsa Malaysia*.

I believe this book will contribute towards that aspiration.

I would also like to put on record my sincerest appreciation to my understanding wife, Samala, for her patience during the relatively few evenings that I spent at home, even after retirement. I also wish to thank Ms Iris Yeoh for typing much of this book, and to my secretary, Ms Haema, for co-ordinating with the publisher, Mr Ng Tieh Chuan, who encouraged me to complete this book.

Tan Sri Dato' Ramon V. Navaratnam

INTRODUCTION

THE rapid economic growth Malaysia has enjoyed since the mid-1980s is a fact that is hard to ignore. This book is about that success and the economic challenges and prospects that lie before us as we march forward into the 21st century.

Consider what foreigners used to say about Malaysia as little as 10-15 years ago, and how things have changed since: Communism may have declined as a threat, said the critics, but racism and religious extremism could still tear the country apart. The government was authoritarian and the economy stumbling along and riddled with inefficiencies. Those of us who lived in the country knew it wasn't true. Of course, there were problems (which country hasn't got problems?), but they were usually blown out of proportion by the foreign media. Some were even invented for the sake of pleasing biased foreigners who did not like to see Asians striving to develop their own societies based on their own values, rather than blindly copying the ways of their former colonial masters.

Today, things are much different. Malaysia still has its critics, but it has also shown itself to be a country that can no longer be pushed around. Some leaders in the United States and the industrial world may not like Malaysia's independent stance and Dr Mahathir Mohamad's proposal for an East Asia Economic Caucus, but it is becoming a reality. Similarly, Malaysia has often spoken up for many developing nations which for far too long have been cowered by the wealthy industrialised West.

Malaysia's economic success is now a matter of statistical record. Economic growth checked in at 9.6 per cent in 1995, a creditable performance by any standard. In fact, things have gone so well in the past few years that the government has allowed employers to bring in more than a million foreign workers to deal with the labour shortage. Economists have expressed concern about inflation, but at 3-4 per cent per annum, it is still very much well under control. Contrary to the doomsday forecasts of cynical critics, ordinary Malaysians have not had it better.

Socio-economic development and human welfare have also made much progress. Consider these statistics: in 1980, there was one doctor for every 3,800 persons in the country. In 1994, this ratio had improved to one doctor for every 2,207 persons. Little wonder then that the infant mortality rate has dropped rapidly and the life expectancy of the population has risen. The general prosperity has also resulted in a remarkable improvement in the number of people owning telephones and cars. Per capita GDP in 1996 stood at US$4,400, almost double the 1990 figure of US$2,311. Unemployment currently stands at 2.8 per cent of the workforce, compared to 6.3 per cent in 1990. In fact, those out of work in Malaysia today are those in the process of switching jobs.

How did this vast improvement in social conditions come about? One reason often given by economists is the government's ability to attract foreign investment despite some negative propaganda. More importantly, however, is the political stability that has resulted from our ability as a nation to work together in peace and harmony—by drawing strength from our cultural diversity, instead of allowing extremists to use this to tear us apart. Furthermore, Malaysia is a democratic country where elections are held regularly and peacefully. This is good for everybody, not just foreign investors. Even the poorest citizen in Malaysia has a chance to select the politicians who best represent his interests.

Of course, choosing the best economic strategy is still very important. In fact, this is something that this book deals with in some detail. We have been fortunate in that the government under Dr Mahathir Mohamad has taken great care to formulate economic strategies designed to reform the economy and make it more competitive. We still welcome foreign investment, though today we have our own big companies working to strengthen the economy, and even investing in Western countries! There is therefore greater scope for joint ventures and other strategic alliances.

One example of a successful government strategy is privatisation. Privatisation, which usually involves public share issues, has had a very positive effect on Malaysia's capital market and has been a good source of new listings on the stock exchange. Experience has demonstrated that workers have also gained from privatisation. The programme has not resulted in layoffs, but has produced wage increases instead. Workers also benefited when the value of the shares they were offered in the newly privatised companies appreciated well above the price they paid for them. Privatisation has also resulted in more competition being introduced into all sectors of the economy. With the privatisation of telecoms, payphones and paging services are operated by other companies. TV3's more imaginative programming have also encouraged the development of our domestic advertising and filmmaking industries. Privatisation of major infrastructure projects is also helping the country pay for the big development projects that will propel the country into the 21st century.

However, now is not the time to sit back and relax! This book points out that there are many issues that require our attention in the years ahead. Over-confidence has its dangers, and we always need to be alert to negative social and economic trends. Corruption is one. Another is the widening current account deficit, and yet another is the continuing problem of drug addiction in the country. We also need to overcome the challenges posed by countries such as Indonesia and China where wages are much lower, by working harder and smarter, and encouraging the development of high-technology industries to replace the labour-intensive industries of the past. But not all the solutions have been found, and we need to constantly strive to build a better future for our children. For they are the ones who will have to bear the responsibility of fulfilling Malaysia's destiny of becoming a fully developed nation by the year 2020.

The purpose of this book, therefore, is to help stimulate public discussion on some of these major issues. It does not claim to have the last word on every issue, but it does aim to encourage a more critical and distinctively Malaysian approach to the problems we face as we strive towards developed-nation status in the next millennium.

The Publisher

CONTENTS

Preface
Introduction

I. Economics
1. The Malaysian Economic Miracle 3
2. The Challenges Ahead 21
3. A Budget for the Future 27
4. Curbing Rising Prices 33
5. New Political Mandate Paves
   Way for New Initiatives 39
6. Balance of Payments Alert 45
7. Economic Vigilance 53
8. Competitive Public and Private Sectors 61
9. Over-Confidence and its Dangers 67
10. Assessing Fiscal Policy 73

II. The 7th Malaysia Plan
11. Promoting Productivity-Driven Growth 81
12. Proposals for Improvement of Plan 87

III. The Civil Service

.13. Professionals in the Civil Service   101
14. Compensating the Civil Service   109
15. Raising Efficiency   115
16. Leadership Ideals for Malaysia   121

IV. Socio-Economic Issues

17. Corruption and Its Dangers   129
18. Environmental Decline   137
19. Listening to the People   143
20. Social Development and Poverty   149
21. National Unity: A Malaysian Indian View   155

V. International Economic Relations

22. Dealing with the United States and Europe   171
23. Lessons Learnt at Osaka's APEC Meeting   177
24. The World Trade Organisation
      and the Third World   185

Index   191

PART ONE
ECONOMICS

1.

THE MALAYSIAN
ECONOMIC MIRACLE

MALAYSIA is a miracle because its success has been, to many observers and especially a lot of foreigners, unexpectedly outstanding. Today, Malaysia is regarded as a Newly Industrialising Country and one of the most successful developing countries. But we know that this miracle did not just fall from the skies. The Malaysian Government and its people have made much sacrifices and worked hard together to bring about this miracle!

Malaysia's economy has averaged a growth of over 7 per cent per annum since Independence in 1957. Inflation has been low at about 3-4 per cent per annum and poverty has been reduced significantly to below 10 per cent of the population. Its income per capita has increased steadily to about US$4,400 whereas its purchasing power is much higher, at above US$8,000. With a population of about 20 million, a land mass of 330,000 square kilometres, and an educated, industrious and disciplined labour force, Malaysia's potential for greater progress is considerable, given its political stability and strong leadership. However, before Independence in 1957, there was much concern and even anxiety that Malaysia would be stillborn, or that if it survived, it would struggle on without much progress, once the British colonial masters left the country. That is why Malaysia's success is regarded a miracle by many!

After all, Malaysia was an agricultural country, with relatively low incomes. It was very multiracial, multireligious and multicultural, with hardly any unifying factor to talk about, except its geographic entity. Even here, the high mountain ranges and deep equatorial forests and jungles tended to isolate communities. Sabah and Sarawak in East Malaysia are separated from Peninsular Malaysia by about 1,000 miles of the South China Sea.

The Malays who composed the majority of the population were mainly in the rural areas. The Chinese were in the tin mines and the towns, while most Indians worked in the rubber estates. The Ibans and Dayaks are mainly agricultural.

The Malays are mostly Muslim, the Chinese generally follow Buddhism and Confucianism, and the Indians are mostly of the Hindu faith. Christianity, however, cut across all races, but enjoyed a much smaller following; the British colonial officers were practically all Christians.

Language varies widely from Malay, English, Chinese, Tamil, to Kadazan, Murut and aboriginal. Of course, besides these there are many other languages and dialects.

Since language is the foundation of culture, it is thus easy to understand why there is such a wide range of cultures that pervade the Malaysian scene. However, there is now one national and official language, namely, Malay, although English is taught and used widely.

No wonder there was so much sceptism about the future of Malaysia at the time of Independence. It is no wonder that even then and long after, there was considerable doubt whether Malaysia would survive, let alone prosper, given such conflicting diversity.

To compound this complicated mixture of race, religion, language, and culture was the Emergency which lasted from 1948 to 1960. The Emergency was really a euphemism for the war against militant communism. This war started soon after the British liberated Malaya from the Japanese, who occupied the country during World War II (1941-1945).

The British together with Malay nationalists and mainly Chinese guerrilla fighters fought behind the front lines and in the jungles, against the Japanese army. When the Japanese were defeated by the Allied Forces, this same Anti-Japanese Army took up arms against the British Colonial Government and the armed forces of the Malayan authorities.

However, after a long, costly and bloody struggle of life and death, the Government forces, together with the British and Commonwealth troops, defeated the militant communists. Malaysia was thus one of only three countries in the world to have beaten militant communism. The other countries were the Philippines and Indonesia.

But there were other reasons for doubt and uncertainty. The British generally felt that only they could govern wisely. Many of their former colonies that had gained independence from the British Raj were getting into trouble. They were dependent on British aid and technical advice, and the British continued to dominate in the business sectors. Few Britons believed that Malaysia could make it without Britain's leadership and management.

Unfortunately, many other Western governments shared this scepsism. How could the ex-colonies of France, the Netherlands, Germany, Belgium and even the United States, ever be able to maintain and sustain the stability and strength, and the wealth and welfare, after their independence. The colonial western powers thought they had brought all these benefits to the South and they thought quite presumptuously that once they withdrew, all these gains could be lost.

Worse still, there were many Malaysians of an Anglophile mentality and loyal to the British monarchy who also had serious doubts about the country's future. They did not believe that, with so much diversity, there could be unity and stability. They also did not believe that the Malays, who at the time of Independence inherited the political power, the civil service and armed forces, could lead and manage the then Malaya effectively. There was also some fear, especially among many non-Malays, that there would be a breakdown of law and order and that the fledgling country Malaya would not succeed for long, as the Malays would overwhelm the non-Malays, especially the Chinese and Indians.

What made Malaya and then Malaysia succeed?
However, Malaya and later Malaysia that was established in 1963, succeeded and proved the sceptics wrong for many reasons. This is the miracle.

In the first place, unlike many other colonies, Malaysia did not really have to 'fight' for independence the way Vietnam, Indonesia or even India did. There was, therefore, a great deal of goodwill towards the British when they left. As a result, their institutions, like the Civil Service, the Judiciary, the Police and the Armed Forces, and the Parliamentary system, remained intact and strong. There was no disruption but a smooth transfer of power.

Senior British officials in all the institutions and the administration remained to serve the country for many years after Independence and provided good training, guidance and continuity to the Malaysians who took over the reins of power and management.

There was no nationalisation of British assets. The corporate business sector which was largely in British hands was allowed to continue to prosper. The British civil servants were given very generous compensation terms on retirement through 'Malaysianisation' so there was no resentment nor destabilisation due to rapid resignations and retirements.

Malaysia was also blessed with an outstanding statesman as its first Prime Minister. He was Tunku Abdul Rahman, a prince, and a lawyer. Most importantly, he was a leader who earned the respect, affection, loyalty and confidence of not only his own people, the Malays, but also the Chinese, Indians, Ceylonese, Eurasians and other races in what was initially Peninsular Malaysia.

It was the genius of Tunku Abdul Rahman, and the leaders of the Chinese and Indian communities, such as Tun Tan Siew Sin and Tun Sambanthan, who formed the Alliance of these three major races and racially-based political parties into one collaborative grouping, called the Alliance Party. This party established co-operation and reduced conflict from the very beginning at the first elections in 1954, even before Independence in 1957.

Even more significant was the genius of the ordinary Malaysian who saw the importance of working together to gain independence and then to ensure that it worked for the benefit of all races. They were blessed with good common sense and the will to survive, or perish through unnecessary conflict. They chose to survive and prosper.

Once the political power was consolidated, it was less difficult to ensure that the country continued to be well managed under conditions of law and order, an independent judiciary, and a fair and reasonable government that was freely elected.

Peace and stability which also ensured the safety of the citizen and the foreign investor and security of property were major factors that enabled the economy to grow and prosper.

Economic Management

The next priority after political independence was to safeguard and promote the economic and financial interests of the country.

On the economic front, Malaysia was blessed with good leadership as well. We had prudent finance ministers, starting with Tun H.S. Lee and followed by Tun Tan Siew Sin, Tun Abdul Razak Hussein (for a little while), Tengku Razaleigh Hamzah and Tun Daim Zainuddin—all of whom I had the honour to serve. We inherited a sound financial system from the British and we built upon it. The Budgets were always well managed. The Budgets were mostly balanced and deficit financing was not tolerated.

In fact, the Malaysian Treasury had a reputation for being very conservative in the early years after independence. With Tun H.S. Lee as the first Malayan Minister of Finance and Tun Tan Siew Sin as the second Minister of Finance for about 15 years, the strong financial foundation was strengthened even further. So much so that the funding for socio-economic development projects was sometimes limited and constrained. This was good in the early years after Independence. Many other developing countries, in the full flush of independence, did otherwise. Political leaders who were not used to handling vast sums of money and the accumulated huge national reserves, happily put their hands into the till to build prestigious projects and even enrich themselves. The consequences were often quite disastrous. Thank goodness Malaysia has been blessed with outstanding Prime Ministers and Finance Ministers who ensured strong fiscal and financial discipline.

Malaysia had always had a tradition of relatively open and free trade. This came from our international market experience in exporting our major primary commodities like tin, rubber, palm oil and timber, even from the early times. Consequently, Malaysia's economic and trade policies continued to be open. Because of this tradition and the generally healthy balance of payments, Malaysia enjoyed liberal Foreign Exchange Regulations. That tradition carried on after Malaysia was established in 1963. This liberal foreign exchange regime continues to this day, and generates much confidence in international money markets.

Unlike some countries, Malaysia treated its business community well. Some countries nationalised the minority community business assets, like in Uganda. In other countries in the region, Chinese businessmen were persecuted and subjected to strong resentment from the indigenous groups. But in Malaysia, the Malaysian Chinese were generally allowed to pursue their business in peace. In the early years after Independence the attitude of the Government was to keep the political and security power with the Malays while the Chinese were encouraged to keep to their business activities. This has now changed.

Malaysia was also always open to foreign investment. There was no antagonism against foreign investment unlike the case in many developing socialist countries like India, Tanzania and Burma. We were very foreign investment-friendly all along.

Socialism and unfettered capitalism never took root in Malaysia. The Malaysian economy can be described as a Mixed Economy, with a blend of some socialist ideals in the area of income distribution and Affirmative Action. On the other hand, there has been managed capitalism to meet the concerns of balance in equity ownership and balanced racial employment, through the New Economic Policy which was introduced in 1970, after the race riots in 1969. The NEP is now incorporated into the National Development Policy (NDP) without the equity target of 30 per cent for Bumiputeras nor any time target for its achievement.

Labour unions were infiltrated with communists during the Emergency. However, as the communist terrorists lost ground and the Government's psychological warfare gained momentum, the unions became more professional and less militant. Relative industrial peace has been the hallmark of industrial relations in the country. This has enabled investors and business to expand and prosper without undue disruptions. Unions have generally been co-operative and responsible.

Economic Planning

Malaysia attached great importance to economic planning from the very beginning. The initial Economic Plan (1956-60) was basically a Development Expenditure Plan. It was primarily concerned with building the infrastructure which was quite inadequate at the time of Independence. The road and railway systems connected only the business and urban centres before independence. But economic planning became more sophisticated as the Harvard University Advisory Group and then more Malaysians returned home with postgraduate qualifications in economics to expand the scope of planning. Malaysia is now in its 7th Malaysia Plan (1996-2000) which is a comprehensive and integrated Macro Plan with detailed sectoral analysis and socio-economic programmes.

It is this kind of socio-economic planning which has given direction and focus to economic development in Malaysia. The private sector has thus been able to make its own business plans within the framework of the Government's long-term planning. This has encouraged longer term planning for the private sector and foreign investors.

These five-year plans have been part of the overall Perspective Plans which cover twenty-year periods or four five-year Plans. Similarly, the five-year Plans are reviewed and revised every $2^1/2$ years in what is called the Mid-Term Reviews. Thus, economic planning is an essential part of economic management. The Economic Planning Unit, which is now staffed entirely by Malaysian professionals, reports directly to the Prime Minister. It therefore has considerable influence and is able to get the full co-operation of all the Ministries and the Treasury as well.

It is just as well that the Treasury is responsible for financing the five-year Plans. In some countries the Treasury or Ministry of Finance and the Planning Agency are under the Prime Minister. There is often conflict between financial stability and economic expansion. Fortunately in

Malaysia this conflict is resolved, more often than not by an Inter Agency Group of officials. This Group is chaired by the Treasury and has representatives from the Economic Planning Unit and Bank Negara Malaysia. Usually, the Economic Planning Unit wants to expand expenditure. The Treasury and the Central Bank, however, would examine the resources available and restrain the planners. It's only when the differences of view are serious that these differences are referred to the Cabinet Economic Committee that is chaired by the Prime Minister. Here the Plans, policies and targets are reconciled and finalised. Then the Plans are tabled in Parliament for approval. Thus there are public consultations and participation. This public endorsement is very useful.

Because of these consultative processes amongst officials, political leaders and the public at large, Malaysia's implementation record has been impressive. Many countries have elaborate economic plans which they cannot implement effectively because they are not related to reality. They are often impractical, simply because the assumptions made for financing and business participation and public support are wrongly based.

It has not been socialism or capitalism but simple, straightforward pragmatism that has been practised and which has paid off handsomely in Malaysia. The economic plans have been realistic and thus, fully implementable. The planning process has been two-way, top to bottom and bottom up.

Malaysia Incorporated

Malaysia Incorporated has been another very important feature of Malaysia's economic success in Malaysia. This concept was first introduced by the present Prime Minister, Dato Seri Dr Mahathir Mohamad who urged the Government and the business community to co-operate closely to promote the national socio-economic goals of economic growth with financial stability and social justice.

There had been mutual suspicion in the past that was derived from our colonial heritage. Businessmen were regarded as purely profit-motivated and without concern for public welfare.

On the other hand, the Government and the Civil Service were thought to be more nationalistic and definitely more concerned with the protection of the national interest and the welfare of the community.

Businessmen were mainly Chinese in the early years after independence. This factor compounded the general suspicion that businessmen are usually greedy and exploitative. It therefore made it difficult for the civil servants (who are mostly Malays) to be empathetic with businessmen.

The Prime Minister, however, narrowed this communication gap between businessmen and civil servants. He promoted the idea that the Government collects about 30 per cent in the form of corporate tax from businessmen. This is used to finance socio-economic development projects and programmes and infrastructure for the poorer sections of the population. Thus, a prosperous private sector will contribute towards building a wealthy nation and provide more revenue, some of which can be used to pay higher salaries to civil servants.

The private sector was also urged not to be purely profit-minded but to also show corporate responsibility by donating to charity and caring for the less fortunate. As more Malay and Bumiputera businessmen got into business, Malay civil servants became less cynical about businessmen. Malay businessmen were also seen to be less exploitative and more caring. The increased collaboration between Malay and Chinese business in privatisation further broke down the barriers between the Civil Service and the private sector.

Privatisation

Privatisation has now emerged as a major contributing factor to more rapid economic growth in Malaysia. The United Kingdom first initiated this idea and Malaysia caught onto it. However, the British seem to have stumbled upon many obstacles in implementing the Privatisation policy. But in Malaysia, probably because we learnt from Britain's mistakes and because Malaysian leaders handled this new and sensitive issue much better, with the employees and unions, we have managed to come out much more successfully than the United Kingdom.

Presently, the major public utilities have been privatised or are in the process of being privatised through the path of corporatisation. Electricity, Telecommunications, Water, Sewerage, Shipping, Ports and Airports, and many major Highways have been privatised. The national airlines and the railways have also gone private. More and more of the Government's over 1000 owned companies and statutory bodies are either being corporatised or privatised. The universities are getting ready for corporatisation while many private educational institutions have sprung up within the context of privatising tertiary education.

Privatisation has saved the Government billions of ringgit and considerably reduces Government employment. More importantly, privatisation has enabled the Government to reduce its expenditures and to cut down borrowing for public investment in infrastructure. A classic example is the North-South Highway which was entirely privatised.

Privatisation has definitely accelerated investment and spurred economic growth. There is no doubt that privatisation will continue to contribute substantially to speedy and sustained economic growth.

The Civil Service

The Civil Service has been a real asset. Malaysia's impressive economic growth owes a great deal to its relatively efficient Civil Service. Government policies, however impressive, could not have been effectively implemented, if not for the strength, stability and ability of the public service, especially at the senior and professional levels. The formulation of policy recommendations for sound decision-making by political leaders, could not have been possible without the high levels of competency of the administrative, professional and management staff in the public service. Unfortunately, this significant contribution of the public service is not adequately realised. This is because the political leaders do not play it up. The public too do not see the top quality of professionalism in the Civil Service, as their dealings are mainly with the lower levels of the public service where standards of service often leave much to be desired.

Economic Structural Evolution

The Malaysian economy has gone through a remarkable transformation in the last 40 years since independence. This has taken place in an evolutionary manner, despite the shock to the system brought about by the racial riots of May 13, 1969.

As a former British colony, its economy was agricultural and export commodity-based. Agriculture accounted for 35 per cent of the Gross Domestic Product in the 1960s while manufacturing had a small share of only about 5 per cent of the GDP. Today the agricultural share has declined to only about 15 per cent while manufacturing has risen to about 30 per cent of the GDP.

How did this major transformation take place? Malaysian leaders and planners realised soon enough that primary commodities like rubber and tin would become less and less important on the world markets. With the strong emergence of synthetic substitutes, commodity prices were prone to wide price fluctuations, which especially hurt the rural populations immensely. The United States Stockpiles of rubber and tin used to play havoc on the state of health of the Malaysian economy. Indeed, the United States could hold Malaysia to virtual economic ransom and create even political problems, if and when it chose to release or manipulate its stockpiles.

Second Stage

The second stage of economic development emerged when the Government decided to diversify its economy. It embarked on an active policy of Import Substitution in the 1970s. Tax incentives were given for processing of Malaysia's raw materials for manufacturing. Rubber, tin, palm oil, timber and agricultural products were provided tariff protection, subsidies and technical assistance, for downstream development, i.e. processing and manufacturing.

Labour was in surplus and so most of the industries that grew in the early years were very labour intensive. This did not matter at that time, as the high absorption of labour reduced unemployment and under-employment, especially in the rural areas where poverty was significant.

13

More employment raised incomes, and enabled access to higher standards of living.

At the same time, massive efforts were undertaken by the Government to open up vast areas of jungle for land development. Farmers who had worked on small, depressed, isolated and uneconomic farm holdings were now given about 10 acres of cleared land for each family, to plant and develop rubber and oil palm estates. This measure had a major impact on reducing poverty and relieving the pressure on the land. Today their land near the towns fetch very high premiums. Many farmers have become rich.

Similarly, the resettlement of over a million Chinese from the jungle fringes to New Villages helped to bring these Chinese farmers and tin miners close to the mainstream of economic activity. Most of these Chinese New Villagers had been exposed to the intimidation and even exploitation of the Chinese Communists who operated in the jungles. Hence, the purpose of the resettlement was to protect them from the communist threat, to deny the communists of their compulsory acquisition of food supplies and money from the helpless villagers and to deprive the communists of information regarding the movement of Government troops.

The New Villages were provided basic amenities such as shelter, water, electricity and land for farming. The villagers also did business since these new settlers were now residents near the populated urban centres. Their incomes therefore rose as their opportunities for business expanded.

Third Stage
With the world recession in the early 1980s, investment in Malaysia declined. The Government realised that domestic savings were not enough to sustain higher investment and economic growth rates. Moreover, the domestic opportunities for investment were limited, especially if they were not export-oriented. The Malaysian market was not large enough to support manufacturing with a population of about 15 million at that time.

So the Prime Minister, Dr Mahathir Mohamad, in another one of his pragmatic policies, gave a series of lectures and made public announcements in New York and in Malaysia around 1985, that the Government would be much more liberal towards foreign investment. This was the 3rd stage of industrialisation.

Foreign Investment

This new liberalism brought in considerable foreign investment and boosted the flagging economy. Investment expanded, unemployment declined, and incomes steadily rose.

The problem of maintaining the balance between Bumiputera and non-Bumiputera investment was also resolved. More foreign investment meant that there would be more Bumiputera investment through joint enterprises. This way the Bumiputera share of the corporate sector could be increased. Otherwise, more investment at the domestic level would imply more Chinese investment. This would have implied less Bumiputera share of the corporate sector and this would be politically unacceptable. With negative political reaction, there would be difficulty in promoting more investment and the whole economy would suffer and continue to be in recession.

This was a clever economic and political move on the part of the Government. The Chinese would also gain from more foreign investment. In fact, many Malaysian Chinese investors joined hands with their relatives and friends in Singapore and Hong Kong and invested in Malaysia, as foreign investors. But who was to know. In any case not many cared. After all, more investment was flowing into Malaysia and everybody gained and was happy. That is the genius of Malaysians' leadership and management styles—its pragmatism.

Foreign investment, however, tended to concentrate on the labour intensive electrical and electronics industries. Malaysia became the leader in the production of electronic components and chips and in airconditioning equipment. But the intermediate component parts were heavily imported. Consequently, the value added was relatively low.

Since so much was imported, the net export earnings did not rise significantly—and considerable strain was put on the balance of payments.

As the balance of payments deteriorated to about US$8 billion in the current account of 1995, realisation grew that Malaysia would have to move up its technology levels to be able to get higher value-added production and exports.

Fourth Stage

Thus, the 4th stage in Malaysia's industrialisation took off with the introduction of the 7th Malaysia Plan (1996-2000).

The thrust of the 7th Malaysia Plan is for productivity-driven economic growth. Science and Technology and Research and Development have been given much greater priority. Total Net Factor Productivity has been highlighted in the 7th Malaysia Plan. Malaysia would now depend less on the traditional factors of production like land, labour and capital but more on technology, higher productivity and the more efficient use of its resources.

World Trade Organisation

This Productivity Approach is timely with the establishment of the World Trade Organisation (WTO) in January 1996. By the year 2005 or thereabouts, the WTO would have exerted sufficient pressure for Malaysia to reduce most of its import duties. By the year 2003, Malaysia as part of Asean and Afta (Asean Free Trade Area) would have agreed to reduce most of its protection of domestic industries. Thus, the Malaysian economy would be very open to competition not only within Asean but also within the Asia Pacific Region and indeed the global marketplace.

Most significantly, if the WTO succeeds in introducing the Trade Related Investment Measures (TRIMs) then Malaysia would be obliged to give National Treatment and National Status to foreign investment. This would encroach on Malaysia's and other developing countries' national sovereignty and national integrity. This kind of WTO pressure will undoubtedly be resented and resisted. But for how long? The industrial countries will use all their resources at their disposal in as many heavy-handed ways as possible, short of going to war, to force their interests through. They have done it before and have had their way. Most countries realise that in a fight between the interests of the North and those of the South, the North wins every time, at least in the short term. The only reasonable and pragmatic strategy is to fight for time and prepare for the worst. In Malaysia's case the problems posed by the WTO onslaught are even more serious.

National Development Policy
Malaysia may have to sacrifice or seriously modify its National Development Policy (NDP) which is the Affirmative Action that gives preferential treatment and protection to Bumiputeras. But the provision of national status would imply giving foreigners the same national status as its own people and especially the Bumiputeras. This would make the continuation of the NDP untenable. If the foreigners are allowed equal treatment, then this equality will need to be provided for the non-Bumiputeras within the country as well. This can be difficult to do, as it would undermine the policy that has brought stability and prosperity to Malaysia. The harmony and balance that Malaysia now enjoys could be upset. The industrial countries need to be more sensitive and less selfish. They must realise that instability can be disruptive and may be to their own detriment as well.

There must be some understanding that has to be established within the WTO to allow non-homogeneous societies like Malaysia which also have Affirmative Action Plans, some special dispensation or exemption from the wholesale and imperfect competitive policies being enunciated within the WTO.

Just as Defence and Security investment is not expected to be given national status under the WTO, similarly, affirmative action policies should be protected against competition for at least some longer and reasonable time frame, during which more sensitive and careful adjustment plans can be made and implemented, with equity and fairness to all concerned. But how will this be achieved?

The 4th Stage of industrialisation would therefore be productivity and technologically-driven, but it will need some protection within WTO, for developing countries that are under Affirmative Action policies.

Information Technology will form the basis for this 4th stage of industrialisation. The Multimedia Super Corridor (MSC) has already been defined as encompassing the area linking up the new Kuala Lumpur International Airport, the new Federal Government Capital City (Putrajaya) and the new Kuala Lumpur Telecommunication Tower. This MSC will provide the thrust for Malaysia's graduation to a new technological era, with high value-added technology and higher earning power.

The adoption of high technology will again be backed by the Government, within the context of the Malaysia Incorporated and the Privatisation policies, and by the business sector. Investment in technology will be left largely to domestic as well as foreign investors. This will be in keeping with the principles of the WTO and also help fulfill the aims of the National Development Policy, since more Bumiputeras would be given the opportunity to be trained to take over the responsibilities of managing the high-technology projects of Information Technology and the Multimedia Super Corridor.

Thus Malaysia will be well-prepared to integrate its economy to the global economy in every way, from low- to high-technology and thus earn pride of place in the new technological era that will unfold in the next century.

Malaysia's Vision 2020

Given Malaysia's continued strong leadership, the genius of the Malaysian people for living and working together for higher goals, despite its unique kind and degree of diversity, I have no doubt that Malaysia will be able to strive for and attain industrialised nation status by the year 2020.

Vision 2020 that was inspired by the Malaysian Prime Minister Dato Seri Dr Mahathir Mohamad is already being actively pursued and realised. Malaysia is on track and on schedule to achieve the goals of Vision 2020.

What is needed is to increase the scientific and technological knowledge and manpower to meet the challenges of attaining industrialised nation status by the year 2020. This is being done through the reform of the whole education system.

We will also need to gradually modify the National Development Policy so that all Malaysians will become more competitive. Only in this way will we be able to integrate into the global grid and succeed. The sooner we do it the better.

But Vision 2020 is not all about attaining industrialised nation status alone. It envisages the creation of a harmonious, united society, bound by strong religious, moral and ethical values, kindness and compassion, a high standard of living and a good quality of life.

Given Malaysia's impressive track record and the strong will to succeed, the spirit of the Malaysian Miracle will prevail and overcome the obstacles along the way to achieve Vision 2020 in about 20 years from now. Then the Malaysian Miracle would reach full maturity.

As we say in the national language *Yakin Boleh*, which means "We Can", "We Will Overcome", God Willing, and take our rightful place amongst the industrialised countries of the world with confidence and greater national pride.

2.

THE CHALLENGES
AHEAD

THE Malaysian economy is facing many challenges. After eight years of consistently high growth of above 8 per cent and relatively low inflation of around 4 per cent per annum, economic strains are emerging.

The economy may not have overheated but it could be heating up. It is like our cars that show the strain when we drive them on first or second gear for a long time. The economy need not run at over 8.5 per cent per annum in the next few years. As our Prime Minister stated recently, a growth of 8.5 per cent per annum is acceptable. After all, how many economies can claim such high growth rates for so long. (The economic success has caused some problems and were addressed in the 7th Malaysia Plan (1996-2000). This plan, unveiled and tabled in Parliament on May 6, 1996, will set new directions in Malaysia's socio-economic growth and will overcome the emerging economic strains.)

What are these strains that need to be overcome?

Inflation

The first challenge is to ensure that inflation is reduced and kept under control. A new special Consumer Price Index (CPI) for the lower income group earning less than RM1,500 per month per household will go a long way to focus on measures to reduce the prices for the lower income groups. The moderated economic growth at about 8.0 per cent per annum will help to reduce the pressure on prices.

Inflation can be aggravated by *inter alia* high economic growth. When economic growth is slow, demand for goods and services is low. Prices consequently are less likely to rise, as consumers have less income to spend. Given our correct choice for economic growth, progress and modernisation, we have to expect some inflation. But have we got more inflation than we can cope with? Will inflation, even at the consumer price increase of about 3.5 per cent, erode the standards of living and cause hardships to the lower income groups? If our current rates of inflation are unacceptable, and I believe this to be the case, then we must do even more than hitherto, to curb inflation.

Balance of Payments
The balance of payments have been weakening. This unhealthy trend is not something new. It has, in fact, been getting worse in the last few years. What is worrying is that the trade account of the balance of payments is also showing deficits. This means that our export receipts are less than our payments for imports. In fact, our export growth is now lagging behind at about 21 per cent compared to the rapid expansion of our imports at about 30 per cent. This trend is not good.

The real problem is that Malaysia's major manufacturing exports are based on a high level of imports. Our electronic and electrical components and products are essentially based on foreign technology. Thus they have small margins of valued added. Put simply, our manufacturing is like the icing on the cake that is imported from abroad. Our own contribution is therefore small. How can we gain much from our electronic manufacturing exports when, for example, for every RM100 worth of exports, we have to import RM90 worth of imported raw materials and intermediate goods? That is why the 7th Malaysia Plan will shift gear in our industrial policies and go for more high-tech manufacturing.

What is worse is that we have even greater losses in our services account of the balance of payments. This includes the large outflow of foreign exchange to pay for foreign shipping, freight, tourism, insurance, education and also consultancy services. This has been a major weakness in our economy for a long time. Somehow, despite several high-powered government committees, this problem has not been adequately resolved. If not for Malaysia Airlines, Malaysian International Shipping Corporation and Engineering and Malaysian Reinsurance, the deficits of RM18 billion estimated for 1995 would have been much larger.

Labour Problems

Labour shortages, especially in skilled workers and professionals of all kinds, constitute a major weakness in our economy. The causes of this problem are manifold. First, the economy is growing rapidly. Thus the demand for all kinds of workers has exceeded supply. Second, the economy is still very labour intensive. We have not been able to upgrade our technology sufficiently fast to move away from the use of relatively inexpensive labour. Third, our education system has not been able to produce sufficient supplies of technically trained workers and scientific personnel. This has constrained us from moving into high-technology industries and exports. It has been a vicious cycle; we want to use high technology but cannot get the skilled workers. On the other hand, indifferent technical workers do not attract high-tech industries.

Low Productivity

Another major weakness is the relatively low productivity of our workers. Some economists will argue that our present high economic growth is mainly due to our large scale use of the traditional factors of production, such as our resources in land, labour, capital and entrepreneurship. We have used a lot of our land, and land resources like tin, petroleum and gas. Our labour has been almost fully employed. With near full employment our lack in labour resources have been liberally supplemented with about 1.2 million immigrant labour mainly from Indonesia and Bangladesh. As for capital, our strong political stability and sound monetary system have enabled us to raise our own savings and even capital through the stock exchange. We have also been able to attract large amounts of foreign investment and foreign private capital. Some entrepreneurial skill we also have. But there are also many top businessmen who have become multi-millionaires because of the special licenses and patronage they have enjoyed. So genuine entrepreneurs are really scarce.

Thus our natural and human resources have been utilised near the limits. Hence, the question remains as to whether we have utilised our manifold resources to our full advantage.

In other words, have we got the full value from the rich resources endowed upon us? Has our productivity been high enough? There are indications that our productivity has been declining. Wages have been going up, but our productivity has not kept pace. We have achieved high economic growth rates largely at the expense of utilising more and more of our scarce resources, rather than raising our productivity.

But there are limits to the utilisation of our resources. If we do not manage our resources well enough, we could run short of land, capital and the natural resources of petroleum, gas, timber and even water and energy in the not too distant future. We should therefore not make short-term gains for long-term losses. We have to think of our posterity. We have to give increasing attention to more sustainable economic development. For this we need more technology.

Low Technology
Technological advances, however, have been slow. This is why the value added in our rubber, tin, palm oil, timber, petroleum, gas and manufacturing has been relatively low. This is the major reason why our balance of payments have been weak in recent years. This is also the reason why some critics claim that our high rates of economic growth cannot be sustained in the longer term. Unfortunately, there is some truth in this argument. We must enhance out technological and scientific abilities to sustain our progress.

Our research and development is still at low levels at less than one per cent of GDP. This compares most unfavourably with more advanced countries where it can go up to 4-5 per cent of GDP. We have a long way to catch up, especially in the private sector where the emphasis is generally on short-term profits.

High Interest Rates

Interest rates have been steadily rising. The base lending rate for commercial banks has been edging up by about 10-15 basis points each time to more than 8 per cent for borrowers. The rising interest rates have been designed to discourage consumption, raise savings and mop up excess liquidity.

The firming up of interest rates has also helped to attract more external funds. This has shored up the ringgit which has been under some strain. The continued weakening balance of payments has no doubt eroded some confidence in the ringgit and caused it to weaken.

However, the rising interest rates could cause the costs of production to increase. This could put pressure on prices and push up the cost of living. We will thus have to watch price increases carefully over the next few months and deal with it more effectively. But it is becoming clearer that we cannot depend too much on monetary policy to fight inflation. We have to do more on the fiscal side as well.

Conclusion

Overall, therefore, 1996 and the next few years promise to be good for the economy. There are, of course, weaknesses in the system that need to be addressed more resolutely if our economic strength is to be sustained. The latest announcement by the Prime Minister that an economic growth of 8.5 per cent would be acceptable, is most welcome. He did not mention accelerating growth by 9-10 per cent which could be counterproductive. Any overheating tendencies in the economy could be dampened by a more comfortable rate of growth of about 8.0 per cent for 1996. The other economic strains are being addressed in the whole series of monetary measures and new polices to reduce the balance of payments deficits. The 7th Malaysia Plan has addressed the several structural weaknesses that I have outlined.

We are therefore all set for a strong, steady and stable economy for 1996, and even beyond. But the prerequisite must be the continuation of strong leadership, sound management and the improvement of efficiency all round. We will need to be even more competitive both at home and abroad.

The challenge now is, how do we increase our efficiency. Although we are a relatively open economy, we have internal constraints that are currently required to protect the less privileged ethnic groups. Competition and affirmative action for the Bumiputeras and Malays can therefore be in conflict. Some of our socio-economic policies therefore may be contradictory. But there is no alternative at present if we want to maintain our socio-economic and political stability. We can face the challenge only by optimising and making the best of our protective measures as envisaged in our National Development Plan (NDP). This is necessary to sustain economic growth within the context of political and social stability.

3.

A BUDGET FOR
THE FUTURE

DEPUTY Prime Minister and Finance Minister Dato' Seri Anwar Ibrahim took the economic bull by the horns in his 1996 Budget Speech. But did he do enough? Was the 1996 Budget up to the people's expectations? On the whole, the 1996 Budget was impressive. It was wide-ranging and pragmatic. It addressed the fundamental issues of rising inflation; weak balance of payments; and caring for the poor, the sick and the handicapped. It was a Budget for the future.

Consumer Prices

However, all the Budget's gallant efforts may not be able to give the necessary impetus in 1996 to solve the economic problems. For instance, the Budget does not give a target or estimate of the Consumer Price Index (CPI) for 1996. It only indicates that the CPI is expected to be "low". How much is "low" is not stated. Is it expected to be below the 3.5 per cent registered for the first nine months of the year?

It has to be. Otherwise, our efforts to obtain a low inflation rate will not be achieved. If we are aiming to attain zero inflation, then we have to be more radical in our approach to dampen inflation. If not, the zero-inflation concept will lose its credibility.

Over the years since 1960, if the CPI has grown by about 3.4 per cent per annum, then in the last 35 years, our cost of living would have more than doubled. This creeping inflation is not acceptable.

Our cost of living is now higher than many countries whose cost of living was higher than ours in the past. I was in Perth, Australia, recently, and I was surprised that the cost of living there is apparently lower than ours. Housing, cars, meat, vegetables and fish are definitely cheaper than ours, even after currency conversion. Dollar for dollar, the cost of living is much cheaper in Perth.

The question that arises is whether the 8.5 per cent economic growth forecast for 1996 is still too high. Although it is still less than the 9.6 per cent estimated for this year, could it not have been planned to slow down economic growth further to around 7.5 per cent? This way the pressure on our cost of living would most likely be reduced. The price for higher growth can be higher prices.

In other words, the CPI may not go down sufficiently lower, unless stronger measures were adopted in the Budget to curb consumption and Government expenditures.

This is why it is a pity that the Sales and Service taxes were not expanded and increased. It would have lowered consumption of the goods and services consumed by the middle and higher income groups. This would have helped to reduce imports of foods and luxuries. Perhaps a later Budget will take it up. The problem is political timing. But when is it really the right time, what with so many elections of one kind or another in Malaysia.

However, the goods and services consumed by the lower income groups could have been exempted from any new sales and service taxes. Thus, the CPI for those earning, say, less than RM1,500 per month could have been protected against any consequential price increases due to any new Sales and Service taxes.

We need to be more concerned with the cost of living of the lower income groups rather than attempting to tackle inflation across the board.

Balance of Payments

With regard to the balance of payments, it is noted that the merchandise account is expected to register a small surplus of only RM1.4 billion. The merchandise surplus has been much stronger in the past. Furthermore, the deficit in the current account estimated at RM17 billion or at 7.5 per cent of GNP for 1996 is still quite high.

It is felt that some of the Government's mega projects could have already been phased out over a longer period of time instead of postponing this important decision. This would have reduced imports for 1996 and beyond. It would also have slowed down the economy and helped reduce inflation.

Some 65 per cent of the RM9 billion of foreign companies' investment income is reinvested locally. Thus more effective incentives could have been devised to encourage a higher proportion of retention of this investment income, to further expand the rate of foreign investment, to help the balance of payments.

More incentives could also have been introduced to expand our shipping, freight and consultancy services. These service industries are domestically based and can be stimulated further to earn much more foreign exchange.

Budget Concerns

The Federal Government's overall budget is estimated to register a surplus of only RM500 million in 1995. This lower surplus may also become a new concern about the economic outlook in the future. The lower budget surplus is, of course, due to the additional RM2 billion for salary revisions in the civil service and a further RM1 billion for bonuses in 1995.

The overall budget surplus could be reduced further, if development expenditure is not held back further. This low overall budget surplus would be undesirable as it will imply the resorting to more borrowing to finance the high development expenditure, if budget overall surpluses are wiped out.

So there could be continuing concern over the high economic growth, the high inflation, the weak balance of payments and now the smaller Government budgetary surpluses despite the new measures instituted in the 1996 Budget.

29

These are some of the major reasons why the local and foreign analysts are taking a cautious view of the outlook for the economy. They tend to think that the Budget package could have been much stronger in dealing with our emerging economic problems. This partly explains the poor performance of our share market. I hope this uncertainty is not compounded by unnecessary speculation on the political front.

But I believe that the analysts' judgements are too harsh. The Government has some strong justification in not having taken a stronger stance in the 1996 Budget, to strengthen the balance of payments and to lower inflation further.

Stronger measures could hurt the economy by slowing it down too rapidly. Then there could be the so-called "hard landing", whereas any Government would like to see a soft landing.

A gradual cooling down of the economy from its present heating up is considered to be more desirable and less disruptive. Businessmen also like a soft landing as business will not be disrupted.

I believe this is a reasonable explanation for the current stance in the 1996 Budget. The Government and the analysts will monitor the economy carefully and tougher policy measures will be adopted if the economy continues to heat up, if not overheat. What is important is for all concerned to have an open mind. We should not be too defensive nor resistant to different or opposing views. Other views may not coincide with our own assessments of the effectiveness of policies to deal with our economic problems. But there can be honest differences in approaches to managing the economy. After all, economics is not an exact science.

Those critics who are ill-intentioned will be found out, but there can be a lot of well-meaning criticism that could be taken up seriously for the benefit of better policy planning and implementation.

Caring Society

But the Budget scored top marks in its strategy to continue the agenda for social development for a caring society. It is gratifying that more and more emphasis is now being given to differentiate between the lower and higher income groups in the application of economic policies.

For instance, interest income on savings and fixed deposits below RM100,000 were exempted from tax. This would benefit the small savers and the lower income groups, as small savers may not be able to keep their deposits in banks for longer than twelve months.

Similarly, the road tax on medium-sized cars of 2,000cc and below has not been increased whereas the higher income owners of cars above 2,000cc will now pay 25 per cent more.

A fund of RM400 million for the assistance of small entrepreneurs has been set up to benefit small Bumiputera entrepreneurs. It is a pity, however, that it does not apply to non-Bumiputeras, many of whom are also in need of assistance.

The promotion of "democratisation through distance learning" will help students from the lower income groups to afford higher education. This is most welcome.

The provision of RM6.1 billion for basic utilities such as water and electricity for the poor is also heartening. This is the only way to assist them move up the social ladder, since the usual tax concessions and incentives do not benefit the really low income groups very much.

It is gratifying that 70 small estates will also be provided basic utilities as these estates could be multiracial. This would reduce the criticism that policy measures mainly benefit one ethnic group. Similarly, it is hoped that the RM75 million provided for Amanah Ikhtiar Malaysia to eradicate poverty could be provided for all our poor, regardless of race, since Amanah Ikhtiar has been primarily concerned with helping the poor Bumiputeras.

Conclusion

The 1996 Budget has laid a strong foundation for the 7th Malaysia Plan (1996-2000). It has been designed to combat inflation and the weakening of the balance of payments. How well the Budget succeeds will depend on how the economy reacts to these new policy measures. The consumers and the analysts will be waiting to experience the benefits of the Budget measures. If the objectives are not achieved and the people's reasonable expectations are not realised, then more will need to be done later, to attain the Budget strategy and sustain economic growth with low inflation.

The Government, no doubt, will also be watching the economic developments very closely to take further and even tougher policy measures to achieve the Budget goals. We must, however, continue to be open-minded, pragmatic and determined to overcome our emerging problems. This is the challenge of managing Malaysia's outstanding economic success. It is not easy. The Government needs the support of all sectors in this exciting mission to continue to succeed.

The issues raised in this chapter are relevant for the Budgets that will follow. No one Budget can address and resolve all the economic problems. What has not been settled in the 1996 Budget will hopefully be taken up by future Budgets.

The 1997 Budget

Now that the 1997 Budget is out, we know that the Government is doing more to encourage greater productivity and efficiency to strengthen Malaysia's competitive position. The measures raised in the Budget will help to sustain the country's economic growth which has now been planned to slow down in order to prevent overheating. This is typical of the pragmatism shown by the Government in its planning.

The 1997 Budget was a solid piece of work although it may not have been very exciting for the man in the street. It did not have many goodies, but it cannot give out too much too often!

4.

CURBING RISING
PRICES

INFLATION is a major concern in Malaysia. Therefore, the Government aims to attain zero inflation. However, the economy has continued to perform remarkably well. Prime Minister Dato Seri Dr Mahathir Mohamad announced recently the dangers of a bubble economy. We are not anywhere near a bubble economy, but we can get close. Rising prices could inflate the economy, which could then burst like a bubble—quite suddenly. But this will not happen because inflation is now under control.

Rising inflation can be the Achilles' heel in our economic progress. It can cause us a lot of problems. Nevertheless, there are still many who ask why the Government is so worried, and why is there so much fuss about inflation? Malaysia, more than any country, must give higher priority to combating inflation.

Why Fight Inflation?
First, we have to ensure that inflation does not cause social tensions which could upset national unity. For instance, the incomes of farmers and fishermen as well as relatively fixed income groups like estate workers and lower level government and private sector employees cannot keep up with inflationary expansion. Businessmen and traders are in a better position to raise their prices and absorb rising prices. But the fixed income groups cannot do much to hedge against inflation. Thus, differ-

33

ent social groups are hit differently. This can cause considerable dissatisfaction and social tensions and could even upset national unity.

Second, the fixed income groups could react to inflation by venting their frustration in their work. They could demand higher wages to compensate for rising prices. Industrial relations could become strained and productivity could be affected. Already wages in some sectors have exceeded productivity and the trend could worsen. All this can undermine our competitiveness. Lower output and rising wages coupled with higher demands for goods and services could increase prices further.

Cuepacs, which is the union representing the lower level government employees, has been pressing for higher wages largely due to rising inflation. Perhaps that is why they have not related their claims to increases in productivity. They deserve a wage increase, but the rate of increase they are asking for is questionable. Wage increases should not exceed inflation and productivity. This will only worsen inflation and boomerang on government employees and other workers. Ceupacs' case could, however, be made stronger if they could show how much more efficient they have become. The long queues at many government departments do not indicate that productivity has increased much.

I hope Cuepacs will spend some time discussing how to raise productivity and performance instead of harping on wage increases alone. Only then can they expect more support from the public and harassed tax payers.

Third, with growing inflation, fixed income workers will find that they cannot cope with rising prices for basic needs like food, shelter, clothing and transport. It could become even more difficult to cater for the needs of their helpless schoolgoing children. Then what would this group of workers do? Most of them will try to cut their coat according to their cloth. The cloth, however, would be shrinking and you cannot wear a shrunken coat. They will try to cut down on food and their basic needs. But there are surely limits to what low and middle income groups (say those earning below RM2,000 per month per family) could do. So, how are they likely to respond? Many will resort to moonlighting, that is taking on another job. This can cause strains in the family. Children would receive less supervision. Discipline could deteriorate and social evils like *dadah*, *bohsia* and criminal activities could increase and productivity would decline.

Fourth, inflation encourages corruption. Both the government's and private sector's fixed income employees could resort to corrupt practices. The bank clerk could shortchange you when he gives your cash. Supplies can disappear from shop stores and artificial shortages could be created to jack up prices.

Ordinary folks could also be affected by corruption. Many of my friends tell me how some policemen were quick to suggest that they be paid a smaller sum of money on the spot, instead of having to pay RM300 for a summons at the police station. They were asked to place RM50 together with their driving licences or drop the money on the ground, to be picked up later! Now we have stricter regulations against drink driving—one hears of even more interesting stories of "drinking fees" being paid on the spot.

There are a growing number of little horror stories not only at the police stations but at the Immigration offices, the Road Transport Department, the National Registration Department and many other places where public services are provided and where regulatory and enforcement systems are in place. The authorities must address these problems effectively to counter the evils of corruption. I wonder how many would dare to exercise their right of citizen's arrest against corrupt policemen. The police could use undercover agents to nab these corrupt policemen who tarnish the image of the whole police force.

There is an economic price to pay for all these criminal infringements. Corruption is wasteful and definitely adds to the cost of doing business. Therefore, it can be legitimately claimed that corruption is one of the causes of inflation. A recent survey by an international magazine rated Malaysia quite high on the scale of corruption among the major international trading partners. This is most unfortunate as it reflects badly on our country and our national integrity.

Fifth, inflation causes distortion in income distribution. Those with fixed incomes cannot keep up with rising prices and soon find their real incomes and purchasing power declining. They are unable to buy the same amount of goods and services as before. Therefore, their standards of living and quality of life deteriorate. On the other hand, some will exploit the shortage of supplies, raise prices and benefit from inflation. The gap between the rich and the poor could widen, and further skew income distribution among the people. This would undermine the Government's aim of creating a more just, fair and equitable society.

Sixth, inflation can also cause ethnic tensions. Groups like farmers and lower fixed income civil servants will suffer most. But if these groups are mostly Bumiputeras, then the ethnic factor could rear its ugly head. National unity and the very objectives of the National Development Policy can therefore be undermined. This, I believe, is one of the main reasons for the Government's concern over rising inflationary pressures.

Seventh, high inflation can also erode the confidence in the value of the rapid economic growth that we are enjoying. It can overheat the economy and cause the economic bubble to burst. Therefore, we have to be cautious about the relentless pursuit of economic growth. Inflation has to be effectively curbed to reduce the threat of any boiling over or bubbling in the economy. Otherwise, the people may get disenchanted with economic development. They will ask what is the use of rapid growth if the poor get poorer.

Solutions

The Government has set in motion many sound macro strategic policies to fight inflation. These bold measures are working. Otherwise, the inflation would have been far worse. However, there are fundamental and somewhat sensitive socio-economic issues that need to be courageously addressed if we are to break the back of inflation.

It is important that Malaysia becomes even more liberal in its policies and more efficient in government implementation and business practices. This will enable us to be even more competitive to produce more at lower cost. Only then will we be able to move more purposefully towards zero inflation and a better standard of living for us all. Zero or lower inflation is therefore not only necessary but also attainable if we work hard at it. However, we should not think that zero inflation can be achieved while we are still enjoying high growth rates. At a zero economic growth rate, we could attain zero or even negative inflation rates. But who wants zero or even very low growth rates?

I have proposed that the government adopt a compromise formula for the CPI. The existing CPI is based on a basket of goods and services that were too general and widespread. Instead, we should have a new CPI based on the goods and services actually consumed by the Lower Income Groups. We shall call it the CPI LIG. These lower income groups could be defined as families or households earning less than RM1,500 per month for an average family of five. Since this new CPI LIG would be made up of all controlled items, that is, food items whose prices are controlled by the Ministry of Domestic Trade and Consumer Affairs, it will not be difficult to give priority to devising policies and programmes that will help keep the prices of such goods and services consumed by the lower income groups down. With such an approach, we could be able to achieve zero inflation for the lower income groups. The original CPI will continue to apply to all consumers—the rich as well as the poor. Management of overall prices for all goods and services could be covered by macro, fiscal and monetary policies.

Wrong implementation of the NEP can cause inflation. The NEP itself will need to be modified to fight inflation. There are intrinsic contradictions between the wrong implementation of the NEP and the fight against inflation. Providing licences to some individuals who may not be able to efficiently run their businesses adds to the cost of goods and services. Restrictive licensing goes against the grain of competition and this causes price increases.

Some licence-holders rent out their licences on an "Ali Baba" basis. The additional rental costs get passed on to the consumers. Therefore, the time has come to be more selective and effective in the implementation of the NEP. Otherwise, we may be helping some Bumiputeras to become businessmen at the expense of the majority who have to pay higher prices and suffer from declining standards of living.

The disproportionate distribution of pink forms can also add to inflationary pressure. While this practice could continue, it would be desirable not to give too much to too few. This practice could cause a situation of "too much money chasing too few individuals". Many of the privileged few will not be able to produce enough goods and services to match the additional funds that have been placed in their hands. Therefore, prices can rise as there will be too much money chasing too few goods.

We have to realise that curbing inflation has to be planned and implemented in a holistic manner. Macro policies must be integrated with micro policies. If anti-inflation policies are considered *ad hoc* or implemented indifferently and separately, then sound macro policies will fail. We thus need to be careful to ensure that policies to curb inflation in fact do succeed.

5.

NEW POLITICAL
MANDATE PAVES WAY
FOR NEW INITIATIVES

THE 1995 election results gave the Barisan Nasional Government a strong mandate for continuity and improvement of its successful policies. But this solid mandate also gives the Government the opportunity to take new initiatives in moving faster towards Vision 2020.

From a business standpoint, there is now a stronger sense of security in investment. The Government's business-friendly policies will carry on for the next few years and also in the longer term. However, it is an excellent time to reflect and ask whether existing policies could be further improved. Do we need new policy initiatives and the implementation of new approaches? Any dynamic economy will call for modifications and changes in policies and directions from time to time. This may well be that opportunity for Malaysia.

Instant Millionaires
Despite our remarkable socio-economic achievement, there are many, however, who feel that higher economic growth rates and better incomes have not benefited them as much as they should have. The big businesses and rich businessmen have gained much more and even disproportionately more than the others. Many became instant millionaires without much effort. Those who do not get the easy access to becoming rich resent the policies and practices which spawn instant millionaires. Policies

could be modified to ensure that more industrious businessmen become small millionaires rather than a few becoming very big millionaires.

Better Government Facilities

The middle and the lower income groups tend to ask why they cannot get more of the same or even better facilities and amenities from the Government. The rural poor would want more allocations for health, education, transport, community development, land alienation, religious centres and recreational facilities. More effort could now be made to distribute the fruits of development. The urban middle and lower income groups ask why more funds are not made available for low and middle income housing and better public health and transport facilities.

Many other areas, although much improved, still give a lot of hassle to the ordinary non-VIP citizen. Even pensioners have been subjected to difficulties when collecting their hard-earned pensions. In the past they could get the pension vouchers through the post; whereas now they have to go to a few selected and preferred banks to update their pension accounts.

Government policies and public services could be further improved to ensure better quality of public services to the lower income groups. VIPs do not experience the hassle because their staff settle matters for them.

Malaysia's record in managing inflation has been good. The rise in the Consumer Price Index of between 3 and 5 per cent per annum for several years is not excessive by international standards. Nevertheless, they are unacceptable. Over the last five years, the prices of goods and services could have gone up by about 20 per cent. On the other hand, wages may not have gone up as much, especially for the agricultural and fixed income groups.

Prime Minister Dato Seri Dr Mahathir Mohamad is therefore giving the right priority to public policy when he urges planners and academics to seek ways and means of reducing inflation to even zero per cent. But are we doing enough to achieve this worthy objective? Is productivity improving fast enough? Are supplies, especially of food and other basic needs like housing, increasing fast enough to slow down rapid price increases?

Fortunately, a much stronger Government will now be able to encourage greater internal competition. This will help it reduce inflation.

The balance of payments has been weakening. Bank Negara Malaysia's *Annual Report* indicates a deficit of RM11.6 billion in the current account for 1994. Fortunately, foreign investment capital inflows for 1994 were impressive at RM13.4 billion. This has helped to counter the negative basic balance of RM11.6 billion in the trade of goods, services and transfer payments. Thus, it is very important that Government policies continue to encourage foreign investment. For instance, any restrictive conditions for high technology industries could be relaxed.

We cannot continue to tolerate the widening trade deficit with Japan. The appreciation of the yen will further burden our debt servicing and worsen the deficits on our overall balance of payments. We should, therefore, deliberately shift our imports away from Japan to cheaper imports from other industrial countries of the south.

East Asia Economic Caucus

Malaysia's economic relations also need to be further strengthened with East Asia and the Pacific. If Japan is not responsive to the East Asia Economic Caucus, then we should modify our Look East Policy. We should get on with the formation of the Caucus, with or without Japan. Japan may join later when it is not too dependent on the United States.

Our vital economic interests are at stake and we must act collectively and decisively to protect them. It is therefore unfortunate that the proposed meeting of the six Asean countries plus three East Asian countries, scheduled at Phuket recently, was not held. Was it because Asean was pressured? Could we not resist this pressure?

Now that Asean is doing well, there is a danger that there would be more pressure from the West on the industrial countries, to divide and rule Asean. They would do this to weaken Asean and erode its negotiating power. They would regard Asean as useful to them as long as it provides stability to the region. But the industrial countries would not want

Asean to compete effectively with them but merely to provide a richer market for the goods and services of the industrial countries.

So they will do more to play one Asean country against the other as they have done elsewhere and in this region in the past. Asean countries have to be alert and united to resist these pressures.

Bank Negara Malaysia's Governor Dato Ahmad Mohd Don has described the Malaysian economy as being "in transition". The balance of payments deficit of the current account is regarded as a temporary phenomenon that is expected to decrease and even turn into a surplus when industries export more in about a year's time.

On the other hand, if the deficits continue to widen the impact on our economic growth, inflation and our ringgit can become unfavourable and even detrimental.

The Government has now even greater strength to take stronger measures to increase our export of goods and especially services.

One important way out of the problem would be to deliberately slow down the Government's and the private sector's spending on the vast infrastructure and construction projects now underway.

Mega Projects

Deputy Prime Minister Dato' Seri Anwar Ibrahim said that some of the mega projects are being carefully paced to avoid bunching. The Economic Planning Unit could monitor these projects and regulate the approval system for new private sector projects, especially commercial buildings, to ensure that there is no glut in commercial space.

Phasing out less urgent projects would lessen the pressure on scarce skilled labour, steel, cement, construction and other materials. More phasing out will definitely reduce the existing bottlenecks. Otherwise bottlenecks could crack, just like bubbles could burst. Slowing down development would also dampen the pressure on wages which are rising unreasonably and inconsistent with productivity.

The Barisan Nasional's slogan calling for Justice and Efficiency is laudable. Thus, the implementation of the National Development Policy (NDP) will need to be modified and further refined to ensure a more level field for competition.

The Poor

On the other hand, more will need to be done to further raise the opportunities for the less privileged and the poor, regardless of race. Their needs are much greater than the rich. The new and overwhelming mandate that Malaysians have given the Government empowers it to take new initiatives to build Malaysia as a model country. God willing we will succeed in eradicating poverty and overcoming our problems, especially under the leadership of Prime Minister Dr Mahathir Mohamad.

The Program Pembangunan Rakyat Termiskin, which is a development programme to uplift the poverty groups through participation in income-generating projects, has been useful and successful. It has benefited large numbers of poor Bumiputeras. Similarly, the assistance given to promote the Bumiputera Commercial and Industrial Community has been commendable. There are many other similar programmes, such as the Amanah Ikhtiar Malaysia which is comparable to the famous Gramin Bank Scheme in Bangladesh. All these schemes have reduced poverty among Malaysians from 16.5 per cent in 1990 to 8.9 per cent in 1995.

But there is no breakdown for these achievements on a racial basis. However, it is well known that most of the aid and advice goes to the Bumiputera poor. Poverty has no racial barriers. The NEP should therefore be closely followed and implementation must ensure that the hard-core poor, regardless of race, must be helped by government agencies and officials. It is unfortunate that if we attempt to give preferential treatment to the very poor based on racial considerations, we will then not be following our national objective under Vision 2020 to be caring.

Strong Mandate

Very few governments in the world have been given such strong mandates to govern. The Malaysian Government now commands a two-third majority in Parliament. This has enabled it to change the Constitution, but the Government has been discreet and prudent. However, existing policies need to be reviewed and revised to meet changing circumstances and the new challenges that we will face.

Governments should govern and leaders should lead. That is why we have done so well. That is why we will need to do better—even if it means changing policies further.

6.

BALANCE OF
PAYMENTS ALERT

AT the end of 1995, Malaysia was burdened with a current-account deficit of RM17.8 billion (8.8 per cent of the GNP), up sharply from the RM11 billion posted in 1994. This burgeoning current-account deficit is indeed cause for concern. The deficit in the balance of payments service account could exceed RM20 billion in 1996. It could deteriorate further and adversely affect the realisation of the aspirations of Vision 2020. This is not tenable. Continuing severe strains on the overall balance of payments could cause serious economic implications, *inter alia*, on economic growth, the exchange rate, the national debt and even national unity.

Investment Income
The bulk of the deficit of about RM11 billion will emanate from the investment income remitted abroad. This is to be expected with the high inflow of capital investment over the last ten years. We cannot and should not want to prevent remittances abroad. However, we can reduce the outflow by providing more attractive incentives to retain these profits for reinvestment. Back in 1969, after the race riots, there was a great deal of capital outflow. The Minister of Finance at that time, the late Tun Tan Siew Sin was asked if the Treasury should consider freezing the outflow of foreign exchange. He replied, "No, over my dead body," and nothing was done. Soon the funds started coming back! The government was

45

right. We have thus always had an open economy. Tun Tan Siew Sin left us a legacy of a liberal foreign exchange system, which has served us well.

The whole range of industrial incentives will therefore need to be reviewed to encourage more reinvestment. However, this is not sufficient. The environment or climate for investment must be improved as a matter of priority. The inhibitions to reinvestment have to be identified and reduced if not removed. Some of these impediments are as follows:

1. The policy of majority ownership for Malaysians although flexible will have to be further improved to enhance reinvestment.
2. The reluctance to approve work permits to foreigners has to be relaxed further.
3. The shortage of skilled workers and professionals has to be rectified by introducing more imaginative training and educational schemes.
4. Higher technology industries and research and development could be given more liberal incentives. It is better to be liberal and then reduce the incentives when our objectives have been achieved, than to deny them now.

Freight and Insurance
A deficit of about RM8 billion for freight and insurance constitutes the second major cause of the high deficits of the service account.

On freight, more competition, more licenses and better equipment, could reduce the amount of freight going through Singapore. There are some monopolistic tendencies that need to be reduced. There should be more competition and less protection in this area.

The shipping industry could be provided stronger financial support and more incentives to expand its capacity. Unless the government provides more incentives and capital investment, this industry cannot be sustained.

The insurance industry has to be strengthened. There are too many small domestic companies. At the same time, the foreign companies have not done enough to restructure. Consequently, large amounts of insurance are reinsured abroad, causing a serious outflow of funds. The danger is that with the World Trade Organisation pushing for more "openness", the foreign companies will now refuse to restructure, or just go slow!

The Government has to take more assertive steps to encourage and persuade the foreign insurance companies to restructure but how this can be done under the WTO is difficult to ascertain. Perhaps we should stall the WTO.

If foreign ownership is to be 49 per cent, then there must be concerted efforts to implement this policy, without exception, but there will be strong resistance from foreign companies. The NDP would be resented, but we need to defend it for sometime yet.

Much progress has been made in banking but the pace of progress is still slow. It will be difficult for us in Malaysia to compete with the giant banks in the industrial countries. That is why many of our banks are merging into larger banks to compete more effectively with foreign banks. But big banks do not mean more efficiency. Small banks that are efficient should also be encouraged.

But it is going to be a different ball game when the World Trade Organisation applies more pressure on us to open up our banking system for more foreign competition. There will be greater strain on the balance of payments then. We have to act now to become even more efficient in our banking.

Tourism

Tourism now provides a net positive balance of about RM1 billion. However, this revenue could be enhanced if there is more support from government-related agencies in the following areas:

1. Improve infrastructure. Malaysia has the potential to be a tourist attraction for locals as well as foreigners seeking that perfect getaway, but there are many beautiful local tourist destinations that are still not easily accessible.

2. Increase private investment in tourism through the provision of more incentives to develop our tourist attractions, i.e. rivers, lakes, waterfalls, hills and mountains, rainforests, wildlife sanctuaries, resthouses, islands and beaches. We will need to think of allowing some changes if we privatise some of these facilities. We could have free access, but compensate the private investors by allowing them to build toll roads and other facilities.

3. Budget hotels can be encouraged through better incentives as there are so few now.

4. Wines consumed by tourists could have lower duties which are now unusually high by international standards. There is no need to impose our moral standards on others. After all, the revenues are not large and can be foregone.

5. The transport system within the country must be improved considerably to attract more tourism. Though the road system has improved considerably, the rate of accidents has gone up tremendously.

6. The state governments and local authorities have to be made more responsible in cleaning the environment and protecting it from further deterioration. It is disgusting for any tourist to have to see rubbish carelessly strewn at our lovely resorts. Worse still, it is terrible to see dirt on white beaches and the destruction of virgin jungles and verdant hills.

Consultancy Services

Presently, about RM2 billion per annum is lost to foreign consultants in professional fees. According to the Asian Development Bank and other sources, about RM500 million is spent just on management consultants in Malaysia.

A large amount of the fees paid to management consultants goes to foreigners because Malaysian management consultants are not registered as a professional group. Unlike lawyers, engineers and doctors, there is no legislation requiring registration. Thus, the profession of management consultancy is made up of self-appointed management consultants who weaken the reputation of the art and science of sound management consultancy. These self-appointed consultants often do not have the proper qualifications and experience and do not perform professionally. So clients lose confidence in local consultants.

The demand for management consultants is estimated to grow by about 15 per cent per annum. However, the professional standards are deteriorating as all kinds of semi-qualified and inexperienced individuals take advantage of this rising demand for consultancy services.

Because there is no proper professional certification scheme, Malaysia is losing out in providing professional management consultancy services to other countries, especially in the Third World.

The World Bank and the Asian Development Bank and other international agencies do not give ready consultancy contracts to professional Malaysian managers because of the absence of professional certification.

The Institute of Management Consultants

Bearing in mind the need to upgrade Malaysia's management consultancy services, the Institute of Management Consultants was formed in 1982 with the guidance and blessings of the then Minister of Trade, Dato Seri Dr Mahathir Mohamad.

The IMC itself is affiliated to the international body of management consultants which held its annual conference in Kuala Lumpur on 28-30 August 1995. The delegates at the conference were impressed with the general standard of our consultants. But they expressed regret that there was no certification scheme that would accord Malaysian consultants higher credibility and status.

Dato Paduka Saleha Mohd Ali, the President of IMC, has requested the Ministry of Finance to introduce some certification scheme for Malaysian consultants. However, the response has been slow. Only if there is some certification of Malaysian consultants, will there be greater credibility and confidence in them.

49

Proposals

Bearing in mind the need to increase the standing of Malaysian consultants and their capacity to earn foreign exchange, it is proposed that (i) the Institute of Management Consultants register all Malaysian management and project consultants and accord them professional status; (ii) form an Accreditation Council comprising of members of the Institute and government representatives from the Treasury, Economic Planning Unit, Mampu and other relevant agencies to give recognition to Malaysian management consultants; and (iii) draw up a list of criteria and guidelines for the Accreditation Council that could use these criteria for the admission of suitably qualified consultants to the Institute.

The Government on its part could help develop the management consultancy profession in Malaysia by recognising the IMC members as professional management consultants and for tendering for Government consultancy contracts. The Malaysian External Trade Development Corporation (MATRADE) could help promote Malaysian consultancy services abroad to earn more foreign exchange for the country.

Conclusion

These proposals, if accepted, will provide recognition of a professional status for Malaysia's management consultants, build greater professionalism for Malaysian management consultants and promote Malaysian consultancy services abroad as well as substitute for foreign management consultants in Malaysia, where appropriate.

The Government has already had several discussions with the Institute of Management Consultants on the issues raised in this chapter. It appears that there is some consensus on the need to establish recognition of Malaysian management consultants. But what is needed now is a definite decision at the highest levels to adopt these proposals as firm policy, as early as possible.

Unfortunately, there is still some colonial hangover in Malaysia. As they say, "A prophet is not known in his own country." Many Malaysians still tend to give foreign consultants more recognition and a higher premium for their services. We have come a long way since Independence. Our consultants are highly trained and experienced. We need not go to foreign consultants for most of our technical work. But we obviously do not appreciate our own talent that is internationally comparable, more readily available and at less cost. This proposal to register our own consultants will therefore be most useful to the profession and the economy as a whole.

7.

ECONOMIC VIGILANCE

THE Malaysian economy has been doing very well but we may now have the problems of success! The time for change and further progress has come. Indeed, Malaysia's steady and strong economic performance confounds critics and pleasantly puzzles even the optimists. How does an economy, especially a developing country, manage to average growth rates of about 8 per cent per annum, with a relatively low inflation rate of below 4 per cent per annum, for eight straight years now?

How is it that so many industrial countries, let alone developing Third World countries, are unable to sustain this high economic growth and low inflation? Some even ask whether Malaysia's outstanding track record is real. Or is there a catch, and how long will this good streak last?

Actually, many countries have failed to perform well mainly because of weak political and poor economic management. Sound economic management requires strong political leadership that steers away from the extremes of both socialism and capitalism.

Malaysia's Economic Management Style

Malaysia's style of economic management takes the middle path. It is moderate and pragmatic. This is our strength and as long as we have a strong Government and realistic policy formulation and implementation, we will continue to do well.

After all, unlike many unfortunate countries, we are blessed with "trainable" human resources and a wide spectrum of natural resources in abundant measure. We also do not have calamities like earthquakes and tornadoes. Given good leadership and unity there is every reason for us to perform well, unless we do ourselves in, but who wants to hurt themselves. However, economic growth and financial stability, although necessary, are not sufficient in themselves for success. Man does not live by bread alone.

This is why the Deputy Prime Minister Dato' Seri Anwar Ibrahim recently proposed developing Malaysia's own unique model of development. We need economic development to fulfil more than our mere economic needs. The economy should actively contribute towards stability, peace, harmony, equity, justice, a clean environment, reward for hard work, enterprise and strong religious and moral values.

In the final analysis, economic progress must provide for a good quality of life, an abiding national unity, a deep sense of individual well-being and an optimistic confidence in the future, as promoted by Prime Minister Dato Seri Dr Mahathir Mohamad in his Vision 2020.

Vigilance
The price for this innovative Malaysian model is vigilance. No economy can prosper without constant nurturing. Mexico thought it was doing well. But it relaxed in its macroeconomic management and see what happened. Mexico's current-account deficit on the balance of payments had been allowed to grow to US$28 billion (RM71.4 billion) or up to 8 per cent of its GDP. This led to heavy losses in its already low reserves, depreciation in the peso, high inflation, low savings and investment and consequently an economic crisis.

Vigilance and Constraints
The moral of the story is not only that we should always be alert to socio-economic changes, but that we should also take timely and preventive remedial action, to prevent the development and deterioration of unfavourable trends. This can only be achieved by greater observance and study of the constantly changing economic and financial scenario.

This vigilance should not be left entirely to government agencies. More private research institutions and non-governmental organisations should also actively participate in economic analysis and commentaries.

The Malaysian Institute of Economic Research is doing a fine job of monitoring and advising on the economic issues and trends, but the universities with their large pool of professors and academicians, could certainly do much more. There should be more public debate and discussion of national socio-economic issues. All this would provide excellent feedback to the Government which would, I am sure, welcome more inputs to its macro planning and management.

MIER expects the economy to grow at a high rate of 8.5 per cent, but estimates inflation to rise by about 4.5 per cent. However, the recent Business Conditions Survey showed a decline, with a fall in production and capital investment.

At the same time, capacity utilisation rose to 87 per cent in the manufacturing sector, indicating that factories will find it more difficult to expand production further, because their machines are almost fully used. Of course the machinery capacity can be expanded, but this takes time as a lot of our machinery is imported.

There is also growing concern that wage productivity is lagging behind. Furthermore, the job hunting sentiment is high with 58 per cent of residents surveyed in the urban areas keen to hop jobs, according to the MIER survey. This adds more pressure to increase wages in order to retain staff and to prevent the pinching of staff. Firms and factories that spend so much time and effort on training their middle-level staff and providing good experience, often lose their staff just for a hundred or so ringgit offered by another employer. This loss causes disruptions and delays on production and lower productivity. Work ethics are changing rapidly with almost full employment and the situation can get worse.

Wage Indiscipline
As Human Resources Minister Dato' Lim Ah Lek pointed out recently, there are growing signs of "arrogance" and "indiscipline" on the part of workers demanding higher wages that are out of line with productivity.

But what will happen if indeed the economy begins to slow down? What will happen when Malaysia fully graduates from its Generalised System of Preferences. Our managers and workers will therefore need to think longer term rather than wanting to benefit in the short term only.

It is suggested that both employers' associations and unions would have to get together more often to discuss more deeply, the strategic longer term implications of increasing wages, declining productivity and rising prices. In the meantime, the authorities will need to do more to persuade the industrial countries that we need more time before we can be considered for exclusion from the GSP. Income per capita is surely not the only or main criteria to be used for exclusion from the GSP. There should be other considerations like the quality of life, the extent of poverty, and educational and infrastructure standards.

We are still far from our aspiration of being an industrialised country. A significant proportion of our population is still below the poverty line (13.5 per cent) and we do not have a strong economic technological base to compete on a sustained basis with the industrial countries. So why should they want to phase us out of the GSP, unless it is due to non-economic reasons like fear of competition and the intention to continue to dominate and to maintain economic hegemony. But what can we do to sustain the present favourable economic climate? The momentum of growth must not be slowed down too much by too many constraints.

Interest Rates
One such constraint could be the rise in interest rates in Malaysia. Recently, our one-month inter-bank interest rate moved in response to the hike in the US interest rates in order to prevent capital outflows. But this can be bad for managing inflation at home.

Malaysia has to keep its interest rates broadly in line with international trends, otherwise we could inadvertently either encourage large inflows or outflows of short term capital or hot money. This could have adverse and disruptive effects on our economy and particularly on our own capacity to manage inflation. Thus, interest rate management at this stage calls for fine tuning. However, we need not follow the US interest rates too closely in the short term. If our interest rates rise too much and too fast, the cost of doing business would rise.

Furthermore, businessmen would be reluctant to expand investment. The stock market could also be adversely affected and individual savings and incomes could suffer. It would be best therefore to refrain from using the interest rate as a tool for fighting inflation and for economic management for the time being, unless international interest rates move significantly out of line with our interest rates.

Manpower Shortages

A major constraint to sustained economic growth is the manpower shortage. We have had full employment for some time now, given that there are well over one million foreign workers in the country. It is just as well, therefore, that the Government has decided to withdraw some tax incentives for labour intensive industries and to discourage the import of labour. These moves would encourage more capital intensive industries and reduce the demand for labour.

But it is imperative that we recognise that there are some critical shortages in the professional and technical fields which are hampering production and restraining further economic growth. Thus the supply and career prospects for engineers and a whole range of technical personnel must be increased on a priority basis if our economic growth is not to be stifled.

What are the Solutions?

First, crash training programmes can be organised to churn out more skilled workers such as electricians, plumbers, masons, carpenters, etc., by the Government. The private sector can also be provided more attractive training incentives to undertake more on site training or even penalised for not providing adequate training.

Second, the recruitment of critical foreign professionals on short-term contracts should be encouraged to break the present bottlenecks, until our own professional output is expanded. These foreign contract workers can leave when our economy slows down. Although the present

policy allows the hiring of foreign professionals, the process is complicated and time-consuming. Part of the problem is that many of our professional organisations have protective closed-door attitudes which make
it difficult for the authorities to expedite the approvals necessary to hire
foreign professionals. But national and public interest should come first
rather than having to consider vested interests.

Third, providing unduly higher wages now can pose serious problems when the economy slows down later. At that time, it will be virtu-
ally impossible to reduce basic salaries. Wage bills will then become in-
flated and could blunt our international competitive edge. This will in
turn cause further economic slowdown and bring about unemployment. That kind of scenario will be unfortunate and must be avoided.

Fourth, more of our womenfolk should be brought into the work
force. It is a pity that many professionally qualified women are forced by
circumstances to give up their careers to mind their children. We will
need to devise more innovative measures to utilise the vast reservoir of
trained and skilled women who are at home, by attracting them to work
on a part- or flexi-time basis. With the rapid introduction of computers
and information technology, we could have our women contribute to
national income and employment by working at or from home.

Fifth, the recent announcement that spouses of foreigners can be allowed to take on employment is most welcome. But the question is
whether our immigration officials would implement this new policy
with flexibility and discretion. We still hear of complaints of inflexibility
and heavy bureaucracy. This must change if the policy is to succeed and
if Malaysia is to benefit from the contribution of good expatriates.

Sixth, the incentives for training and the upgrading of skills have to
be increased substantially, if more employees are to be enticed into
higher levels of training and career improvement. Tax concessions for
training will have to be reviewed, revised and made more attractive. The
government will have to provide higher starting wages and better career
prospects for the professions like engineers and technicians, where
graduates are in short supply. Although in the long term market forces
will resolve the wage differentials and the output of technical graduates

from local educational institutions, the government could hasten the process of adjustment within the public service. The private sector then will also follow suit expeditiously. Otherwise, the private sector will drag its feet and the supply of more technically qualified manpower will continue to slow down.

Given that our economy has been growing for eight long years now, it will be most timely to review our policies, and rethink and revise our plans, to prepare for the new socio-economic challenges of the 21st century.

The 7th Malaysia Plan has done some reassessment of our performance and our direction. But we will have to continually review the economic and financial scenario. This is because the world economy is changing so fast. One area where we need to be especially concerned about is the threat posed by the World Trade Organisation's pressures to open up the Malaysian economy, even if we are not yet ready to do so.

8.

COMPETITIVE PUBLIC
AND PRIVATE SECTORS

ECONOMIC efficiency must be more actively sought in order for it to be ingrained in our Malaysian work ethic and culture if we are to attain the socio-economic objectives of Vision 2020. Both the public and private sectors must be even more competitive for Malaysia to progress further. Otherwise, the prosperity that we all now enjoy could diminish.

It is, therefore, gratifying that the Malaysian Prime Minister, Dato Seri Dr Mahathir Mohamad, and the Chief Secretary to the Government, Tan Sri Ahmad Sarji Abdul Hamid, have been relentlessly championing the cause for more efficient and improved Government services to the public. A whole range of Government circulars and guidelines has been disseminated urging civil servants, especially those at the counter level, to serve the public more politely and promptly. Consequently, the standard and quality of counter service has certainly improved in the last few years. There has been a greater awareness to serve the public better after the Client's Charter was introduced. But what is the actual degree of success of all these laudable initiatives by the Chief Secretary?

We can only find out if we monitor the quality of service to the public. Thus, the Government could consider privatising Customer Service Surveys in every major front-line department. These surveys would give valuable feedback to the top managers in the civil service on the effectiveness (or otherwise) of their staff in serving the general public. The survey results could also be made public so that the efficient departments could be given credit while the weaker ones could be urged to improve. As it is, only the best departments are recognised with quality awards while the rest of the public service carry on as usual, perpetuating their poor performances. This would not be fair to Government policies and efforts to provide quality service to the public.

Public Complaints

It is in this context that the initiative by the Public Complaints Bureau's Director-General Ng Kam Chiu is most welcome. He plans to send investigating officers directly to government agencies to resolve problems of delays and deficient service to the public instead to writing letters and sending reminders. Now he promises quarterly reports—this is most heartening. This dynamic approach in public administration will certainly cut red tape and give the public more confidence in dealing with Government departments. I really hope so—for the sake of the Government and the people. But why is the Bureau relatively quiet now?

Unlike in the private sector where the consumer can change his bank or transfer his patronage to another shop for better service, dealing with Government departments sometimes is like dealing with monopolies with all the attendant problems. Perhaps the bureau could publish a list of complaints that it receives for different departments and indicate what proportion of the complaints were solved and within what timeframe. This would encourage the majority of civil servants who are good. It would also help identify and urge the small minority of civil servants with a *tidak apa* attitude to strive harder to serve the public and the nation. Let us encourage more competition at the counter service level so that the public can be saved much hassle. Tardy staff should be disciplined.

Private Sector Ineffectiveness

But the private sector too poses problems. There are some doctors who are apparently posing as specialists. Thus, they could be providing poor services at unduly high fees. Tan Sri Dr Abu Bakar Sulaiman, the Director-General in the Ministry of Health, reportedly calls them "bogus specialists". If professionals like these doctors can practice cheating, then they are no better than some unscrupulous businessmen to whom these doctors should have set a better example. It is therefore just as well that the Ministry of Health is planning to register specialists separately. However, it is also hoped that the registered specialists will have the proper qualifications for their specialities. Measures such as these that are taken to curb abuses will also help to combat unfair trade practices and inflation due to unfair pricing by doctors!

Health can be adversely affected by pollution from excessive smoke emitted by motorised vehicles. Patients with respiratory problems have to spend more on medical expenses. These expenditures could be reduced if there were better enforcement by the relevant authorities. Thus it is good news that the Deputy Minister of Transport announced that the police and Road Transport Department will continue to rely on photographs when booking vehicles emitting excessive smoke. Stronger enforcement through regular monitoring is necessary for a cleaner environment and better health. Unnecessary medical expenditure leads to budgetary strains and unproductive use of scarce resources which in turn exert pressure on prices and cause inflation.

Shame on those companies which are not complying with the environmental regulations of the Department of Environment (DOE) and congratulations to the DOE for resorting to publishing a list of errant companies and even taking them to court. How irresponsible can these companies (even large corporations) be? It is good that DOE is finally taking a tougher stand. Its enforcement officers should be commended and not criticised for their salutary action.

Publicising Errant Companies

I suggest publishing a list of errant companies repeatedly and even persuading the mass media to feature photographs of the chief executives of these recalcitrant companies that are deliberately damaging our environment and eroding our health and economic resources.

Furthermore, this is the opportunity for our consumer movements, environmentalists and other civic groups to rally round the Government in its campaigns to protect our heritage and environment. In fact, why shouldn't these groups boycott the products of these errant companies? Why can't they organise peaceful picketing for a good cause—with, of course, the proper permits to protest?

The purely profit-oriented businesses must be made to realise that they have an obligation to society and posterity as well. The Government should openly pull up these irresponsible companies. We do not need them.

Foreign competition will soon threaten Malaysia's service sector, which is in for a major review and revamp. This will come about with the World Trade Organisation taking over the regulation of international trade in services such as banking, shipping, freight insurance, intellectual property and professional areas like law, stockbroking, etc.

The British Chancellor of the Exchequer, Kenneth Clarke, realising the golden opportunities for business in the Malaysian service industries, had offered to develop Malaysia as an alternative financial centre to Singapore. Well, we could tap the British expertise but we should also keep avenues open to other world financial centres like New York, Tokyo and Frankfurt. But more importantly, we should start now instead of waiting any longer, to determine and define our liberalisation policies and plan more specifically, as suggested by the Deputy Prime Minister and Finance Minister Dato' Seri Anwar Ibrahim. The earlier we get ready the better.

This would enable the private sector to better prepare itself to open up more speedily and effectively to face the new challenges of foreign competition in the sector within an acceptable time-frame. If we do not plan purposefully early enough, we will lose out, when the pressure for more competition mounts and when we are obliged to open up further.

Housing

Inadequate low-cost housing has been a major problem for a long time. Now our Prime Minister Dato Seri Dr Mahathir Mohamad has justifiably criticised the abnormal price increase of 30 per cent in house prices in the Klang Valley. He attributed this to speculation and other factors.

The solution to the problem is to increase competition among developers by making more suitable land available for low- and medium-cost housing. The authorities could alienate more State land, or better still, the Government could set up a Housing Authority that could acquire land in the public interest at fair market prices to beat the speculators. The housing authority could then build the low- and medium-cost houses and sell them at a reasonable profit to the public. I wonder why it has taken so long to establish this Housing Authority. This way, more low- and medium-cost houses will be built to benefit those in the lower income group. Land is a major cost factor but other costs such as cement, steel, equipment, etc. could also be reduced through more liberalisation and competition. The long-standing housing problem can be overcome if we follow the Prime Minister's lead in giving it greater priority and commitment. We need to solve the housing problem now. A bold new policy and thrust for more housing would therefore be most welcome. (The government has now addressed this issue in the 1997 Budget.)

Indeed, a bold move was made recently with the government's announcement that low-cost housing would be undertaken mainly by the private sector from now on. While the state governments and state economic development corporations have and can build low-cost houses, their track record has been dismal because they are unable to benefit from cross-subsidisation from the high-cost housing (undertaken by the private sector) to the lower-cost housing which is hardly profitable. State governments therefore have had no financial incentives, other than political, to build low-cost houses. Furthermore, many state governments and State Economic Development Corporations have little land left near the urban areas, as these lands are mainly in the hands of private developers. Thus building low-cost houses far way from the urban centres of employment are even less attractive.

Thus only 29 per cent of the total of 800,000 new housing units have been allocated to the public sector for completion under the 7th Malaysia Plan. But 71 per cent or 570,000 units, including 140,000 low-cost units, have been allocated to the private sector under the 7th Malaysia Plan.

These targets are fine, except that the private sector will need to be given more incentives to meet these targets, particularly the need to cut out the considerable red tape that has practically strangulated initiatives for the private sector to do much more to provide more and better low-cost housing.

The ceiling price of RM25,000 per low-cost unit is unrealistic. It was fixed many years ago and is reasonable only if land costs are nominal. (This price has now been modified.) Unless these policies and procedures related to low-cost housing are radically revised, the prospects of realising a house-owning democracy will remain just a blueprint. The government therefore needs to act more resolutely because the demand for housing is expected to increase due to an expanding population. During the 7th Malaysia Plan period, the population is estimated to grow at an average annual rate of 2.3 per cent to reach 23 million by the year 2000.

The Federal Government (which is under the Barisan Nasional) should take the errant Barisan Nasional Chief Ministers and State Governments to task if they do not fulfill their housing targets and obligations to the people. How could we allow private developers to ignore their commitments under the conditions of the developers license, to build low-cost houses. Surely these errant private developers should be penalised. Can't the Barisan Nasional Government pull up the Chief Ministers or Menteris Besar who are in Barisan Nasional, for not disciplining the errant developers. The people expect their representatives to look after their interests first.

9.

OVER-CONFIDENCE
AND ITS DANGERS

AS we stride confidently into the future, we are bound to ask questions as to whether we are justified in our confidence of our country's economic outlook and prospects. But more specifically how will we fare as individuals and families? Will our incomes rise? Will our jobs be secure and satisfying? Are there any warning signs to take heed of lest we get unduly complacent and over-confident? No one wants to be caught unawares, especially when our own well-being can be adversely affected.

However, it is encouraging that the latest international economic indicators from the International Monetary Fund continue to show steady growth, better employment prospects and relatively low and stable inflation in the industrial countries.

We can therefore expect the Malaysian economy to be buoyant with growth around 8.0 per cent and almost full employment in the near future. Incomes will rise as increments and bonuses increase. Job-hopping will continue as employment opportunities abound. Employees will become more demanding, salaries will become more competitive to prevent staff from moving—but productivity may not rise correspondingly.

However, at the lower levels of employment, our own workers could be displaced by less expensive and generally more productive foreign workers, with over one million of them around, able and willing to take on any job without being too choosy. Unless therefore our skilled workers from the *kampungs*, new villages, estates and the urban dropouts are prepared to take on the tough jobs or upgrade their skills, our workers could find themselves ironically unemployed, underemployed and contributing to the ranks of the idle and aimless. Thus we could have increasing social problems and decreasing productivity for our labour force. This low productivity could be tolerated in the short term but economic growth will be undermined in the longer term.

Prices will be rising faster. The Budgets are not clear about the inflation forecasts but the CPI will rise to about 4.0 per cent. This will be a jump from the average of around 3.6 per cent.

If the CPI is to increase significantly, then the prices of food can be expected to rise to about 6 per cent. This is not healthy since the lower income groups who spend a higher proportion of their small budgets on food, will suffer more than the higher income groups. This in itself will aggravate the gap between the rich and the poor and social tensions can increase.

Controlled Prices
Some major food items have their prices controlled. But does it work? Controlled prices can be ignored by cheating on weights, and providing poor quality goods and services. Sometimes surcharges are made for transporting goods to remote or rural areas. Controlled prices are also not observed in areas where the enforcement authorities are out of reach. Here again the lower income and rural groups would be more adversely affected. The effectiveness of controlling prices is therefore questionable. Contractors complain that they do not always pay the controlled price for cement but have to pay extra. Housewives will tell you that they have to pay more than the price tagged for chicken by paying extra for the chicken feathers!

The CPI also includes those controlled items in the basket of goods that are also used to measure price changes. Perhaps the CPI basket could exclude the controlled items to show the price changes of the non-controlled items separately. This proposed additional CPI could be termed CPINCI (Consumer Price Index for Non-Controlled Items).

Thus consumers would be able to relate more realistically to this new index, as it would be more reflective of actual prices in the marketplace.

Wages and Productivity

Wages are part of the cost of production. If wages go up, producers pass on the extra costs to consumers as businessmen try hard to maintain their profit margins. With more competition, which should be actively encouraged by the authorities, profit margins could be narrowed. But there is a limit to squeezing profits and returns on investment. The ideal solution would be to keep wages from rising too rapidly and especially in line with increases in productivity. But how is this to be done?

The co-operation of the trade unions becomes vital. But all the exhortations to have flexi-wages that are related to productivity do not seem to have gained much support in the past. It is therefore reassuring that after three years of unfortunate delay, the technical committee of the National Labour Advisory Council on Wage Reforms did meet. The widening gap between increases in wages and productivity is alarming. How else can we describe productivity increase in the manufacturing sector at 2.2 per cent per worker as compared to wage increase amounting to 11.5 per cent! How can the manufacturing sector continue to be efficient and competitive if this wage output gap widens further.

According to the Ministry of Human Resources, overall wages have outpaced productivity by about 7.0 per cent. This is bad news for our aspirations to build up competitiveness and to sustain high levels of export and economic growth. How can we compete with the lower costs of labour in Indonesia, Thailand and indeed with most other developing countries? We could easily be outpaced and foreign investors could easily be attracted to the lower cost and abundant supply of labour in many countries around us.

It is therefore hoped that good sense will prevail. Labour, employers and the Government will need to have heart-to-heart discussions to work out fair and reasonable guidelines and reforms that link wage increases to productivity. This is necessary for the long-term interests of all three partners and for the future progress of our society as a whole.

The recent relevant principles for wage reforms announced by Minister of Human Resources Dato' Lim Ah Lek, which relate wages to productivity, are therefore very encouraging. The guidelines provide a sound basis for further discussions, which hopefully would lead to the adoption of some consensus on these guidelines which could then be implemented as early as possible to enhance our national competitiveness. These wage reforms should be structural in nature and not be subject to short-term, *ad hoc* and self-centred considerations. This is why the recent proposal by the Malaysian Institute of Economic Research (MIER) to introduce anti-poaching legislation is questionable. Too much regulation can cause other problems and unnecessarily interfere with market forces. We should not be treating the symptoms but the causes of these poaching problems, which are quite serious.

Instead the Government could step up the output of skilled workers and also improve the technical content in the school curriculum and enhance the attitudes to technical studies and occupations. It must be realised that our students may not be attracted to the technological and scientific studies, if our scientists, engineers and blue-collar workers are not paid much more than those with general education and with liberal arts degrees. This is where the Government can set the lead for the private sector, by improving the salary schemes for the technical and professional staff.

Malaysia's Ranking

Malaysia shares with Indonesia the fifth place in Asia where multinational companies prefer to invest, according to a survey of 1,000 global companies conducted by the international accounting firm of Ernst & Young. China comes out top with 70 per cent while Malaysia scored 53 per cent after Thailand's 57 per cent, Hong Kong at 64 per cent and Singapore at 61 per cent. This survey is not encouraging as Malaysia, I would have thought, should be well above Indonesia and Thailand.

But assuming this is a reasonably accurate international assessment, then we have to be concerned that global perceptions of Malaysia are either changing or have changed without our knowledge.

70

It is indeed useful for us to take note of what others think of us, otherwise there is a danger that we may believe what we like to, instead of what the reality is.

We cannot, therefore, be complacent and take our current economic success for granted. Other countries are moving fast and becoming more attractive. They will surpass us if they are able to attract foreign investors more successfully.

Our policies, practices and productivity, including the cost of labour, should therefore be constantly reviewed to keep us more competitive in the future, otherwise we could slowly lose out to our emerging neighbours and competitors.

Index of Economic Freedom

On the other hand, the prestigious Heritage Foundation in Washington has placed Malaysia in the 15th place out of 101 nations in its Index of Economic Freedom. This is very laudable. The index describes Malaysia's low barriers to investment, moderate tax rates and moderate restrictions on banking as attractive for foreign investors.

This Index of Economic Freedom could be enhanced by the recent agreement among employers and employees to have guidelines on wages and productivity. The Minister of Human Resources has succeeded in getting this agreement accepted, but it is hoped that it will work effectively. Both employers and labour need to work closely together and collaborate for mutual benefit on the basis of a Smart Partnership if Malaysia is to continue to sustain its momentum of growth.

The conclusion that can be drawn is that although Malaysia continues to be attractive for foreign investment because of its economic freedom and liberalisation, some of its lustre may be wearing out because of the potentially larger market and wage competitiveness in countries such as China, Indonesia and Thailand. We will thus need to work harder and smarter in the years to come, otherwise what is in store for us may not be as favourable.

10.

ASSESSING
FISCAL POLICY

THE Malaysian economy has performed impressively, largely because the Minister of Finance and the Treasury have consistently upheld high standards of fiscal management. Financial prudence and discipline have been the hallmarks of Malaysia's fiscal and monetary policies.

The 1995 Budget is typical of this fiscal discipline. It is here taken as a case study of how Malaysia manages its fiscal policies. Indeed, this case study can be applied, in principle, to all Malaysian Budgets.

It is clear that the 1995 Budget was bold, comprehensive and caring. Bold because there has never been so much revenue, amounting to about RM2 billion, foregone in any single Budget. Nor has there been such wide coverage of so many sectors of the population that gained so much in concessions. The small- and medium-sized industries got a big boost with the establishment of a Domestic Investment Fund of RM1 billion. This would comprehensively cover all small businesses, including the Bumiputera Commercial and Industrial Community, for which another RM678 million was provided.

All this would help to strengthen the sinews of Malaysia's own entrepreneurs who could provide supplies to multinationals. Otherwise, they would continue to import intermediate goods and services, much to the detriment of promoting greater domestic technological development.

Low-cost housing was provided another RM400 million to raise the new revolving fund for housing to RM1 billion. The total allocation for low-cost housing is thus now RM2.6 billion.

The question is whether the public sector can deliver. Perhaps the public sector should be given lower targets while those of the private sector could be increased—with more appropriate support from the Government.

Public sector housing could be privatised even more to get faster results to benefit the low-income groups. This approach would also help to eradicate poverty more efficiently and expeditiously.

Low-cost housing will definitely get a much-needed boost if the ceiling of RM25,000 can be raised in places where land costs are higher. Also, State Governments could help much more by providing more suitable land at more reasonable and affordable prices.

Priority for the Poor

The poor were given priority in that RM9.2 billion or 64 per cent of the total development expenditure of RM14.4 billion was allocated for rural projects that would benefit those in the *kampungs* and presumably those in the new villages and estates as well.

It is quite remarkable that the rate of poverty will be wiped out in the next few years. The will is there and the way can be found to take the bull by its horns, but it must be sustained to succeed!

No taxes were raised presumably in any Budget for the first time. But it is not reasonable to expect "no tax budgets" as a trend in the future. Neither is it possible to rely on reducing taxes to combat inflation.

Taxes can only go down if development expenditures are curtailed or privatised, otherwise it will be necessary to have to borrow to finance infrastructure. and we do not want to restrain development expenditure too much.

Consumers will gain from the cutbacks in 2,600 items of imports.

About 800,000 civil servants will gain from the bonus and 380,000 taxpayers or 30 per cent of the total tax payers will now not have to pay income tax.

Actually, the 1995 Budget need not be inflationary. The RM2 billion foregone in taxes includes the reduction in import duties that could lower the prices of imported goods, through increased supplies and greater competition. But more importantly, the causes of rising costs, including the constraints to increasing supplies and productivity, must be more seriously studied, identified and reduced or eliminated. Fewer rules and regulations will lead to freer trade, which will bring about greater competition. This is a prerequisite to reducing prices.

More competition means more efficiency in the production of goods and services. This would increase supplies and dampen price increases. Competition can be enhanced only if protection and subsidies are further reduced.

Future Budgets and public policy could aim to reduce protection even more speedily so as to more effectively combat inflation and even bring it down to zero or near-zero levels.

The 1995 Budget is expected to have an overall surplus of RM543 million. This record of recent budgetary surpluses is almost unique in that it is internationally a rare fiscal phenomenon. However, for 1995, the estimated surplus is based on a shortfall in the development expenditure by about RM2.5 billion from an appropriation of RM14.4 billion. This could be the reason for the large budget surplus.

Bonus for Civil Servants
Since the RM1 billion bonus for civil servants is to be paid this year, the 1995 Budget will be spared the strain. But if the implementation capacity for the development budget improves significantly, then the shortfall will be less and the prospects of an overall 1995 surplus could be adversely affected. But unfortunately, such a large shortfall indicates slow implementation and delays in the completion of infrastructure projects.

If the Budget during the course of 1995 is not able to attain its planned overall surplus, then development expenditures will need to be further slowed down or phased out over to 1996. Alternatively, the allocated development targets can be achieved and financed by borrowing, as the Government's external debt servicing is still low at about 1.4 per cent.

As long as the overall 1995 Budget outturn is approximately in balance in the medium term, there should not be a need to slow down on infrastructural development.

Hopefully, the Malaysian economy will continue to boom with the improving performance of the industrialised countries. This will enable government revenues to expand further and help finance the rapidly-growing development expenditures which are required to strengthen Malaysia's rapid socio-economic progress.

Malaysia's prospects for sustained economic growth and price stability could be further strengthened with the more liberal stance taken by APEC for the future.

It is just as well that our Prime Minister, Dato Seri Dr Mahathir Mohamad, was able to get APEC members to agree that the target dates for the reduction and elimination of tariffs should not be binding. Otherwise, Malaysia would have had to meet some unrealistic targets and this could cause disruption to the steady and sustained growth that we have experienced.

Tariffs must and will be reduced, but this must be done in a carefully-planned and gradual manner that would take into account our own social, economic and national interests.

The EAEC

This brings us to the need to push for the early establishment of the proposed East Asia Economic Caucus. The EAEC could accelerate the prospects of greater international trade and investment amongst countries in the Asia-Pacific region in an equitable, harmonious and stable environment. It is therefore timely to step up efforts to establish the EAEC.

The East Asian economies have their own special needs as developing and industrialising countries. These would be very different from those of the industrialised countries. Unless the East Asian economies can consult early and get their act together, it is likely that the APEC meeting will put more untimely pressures on the developing countries to

76

comply with the interests of the stronger industrialising countries. It is useful to start the planning process now so that prospective EAEC members can meet often enough to prepare for the APEC meetings that will follow.

PART TWO
THE 7TH MALAYSIA PLAN

11.

PROMOTING PRODUCTIVITY-
DRIVEN GROWTH

THE 7th Malaysia Plan (1996-2000) will be Malaysia's last socio-economic five-year plan for this century. It lays the foundation for the new century and it is therefore a momentous plan. It is a document that must be read or we must at least be aware of its major issues and implications as the plan will affect our lives.

Economic planning has worked remarkably well in Malaysia. The experiences in many other countries have not been as encouraging. They have planned but not been able to deliver.

In Malaysia, we have the Economic Planning Unit, the Treasury and Bank Negara Malaysia that form the Inter Agency Macro Planning Group (IAPG). This group initiates planning, reviews the performance of the plans and revises them as they are implemented. This way the plan is dynamic and serves to reflect the changes occurring in the economy and makes the necessary adjustments.

The 7th Malaysia Plan is by definition only a plan. It does not contain much detailed policy measures, programmers and projects. The plan presents the broad canvas for the future directions that the economy must take, to reach the goals and aspirations of Vision 2020. It is the annual budget that will translate the policies into projects for which detailed expenditure allocations will be made.

So, what is new in the 7th Malaysia Plan? Is it more of the same, like the 6th Malaysia Plan (1991-1995) and the plans before. Yes, there is much that is the same. High economic growth with price stability, more equitable income distribution, alleviation of poverty, the restructuring of society and the creation of a Bumiputera Commercial and Industrial Community (BCIC), are all not really new issues in our economic planning. It is the emphasis that has changed with each new plan. But the 7th Malaysia Plan is different.

Economic planning has been a major feature in our economic management soon after Independence. The British colonialists were not interested in long-term planning because they realised after World War II that they had to leave sometime. So why plan for others to benefit in the longer term, when they would not be around to enjoy the fruits of their labour. It was the Malaysian civil servants who took up the challenge after *Merdeka*.

Planning has mainly aimed to promote economic growth, price stability and the alleviation of poverty. Basic infrastructure was necessary to achieve these objectives. In the early days of our Prime Ministers, Tunku Abdul Rahman, Tun Abdul Razak Hussein and Tun Hussein Onn, the emphasis was on raising rural incomes and the standards of living. Then we gradually moved on to developing our infrastructure for greater industrialisation, especially under our present Prime Minister, Dato Seri Dr Mahathir Mohamad. But the 7th Malaysia Plan does the same and even more. It charts new directions for the economy to pursue.

Raising Productivity

The real new thrust under the 7th Malaysia Plan is to raise productivity. We have been doing very well by utilising and managing our natural and agricultural resources effectively. Abundant land, previously surplus labour, adequate capital due to our high savings, together with our rubber, tin, palm oil, petroleum, timber and natural gas, have all helped us to prosper. But there is a limit to what we can achieve, to sustain our higher growth rates, high employment and rising incomes, based on prudent management of resources alone.

We now need higher Total Factor Productivity (TFP) to continue to prosper. Malaysians must get used to this economic concept in order to understand this new policy thrust, so as to be able to contribute more meaningfully to our future progress. Total factor productivity, a key indicator of economic efficiency, reflects the optimal use of labour and capital resources. It refers to the marginal output generated as a result of the introduction of new technology or upgrading of technology, innovation, improved management techniques and the enhancement of workers' skills and education.

What then must we do to attain higher productivity? The urgency of increasing our efficiency and productivity becomes imperative with the external pressures building up from the Worth Trade Organisation. The WTO will force Malaysia to reduce and eliminate all forms of protection of our industries. We will have to open up our economy more rapidly to competition from outside. We will even have to allow foreigners to come into our country and compete with us in our own backyard. We therefore have to be much more efficient to compete with the best from all over the world.

But how can we raise our competitiveness? We can, if we have the determination and the stamina. Currently, the major impediments to increasing our efficiency are our own policies, lack of skills, relatively weak productivity and inadequate entrepreneurship.

Modifying the Education System

In terms of policy, we have to modify our education system. We have to make it more technologically- and quality-oriented. In the past we have emphasised quantitative—not qualitative—education. It is time we remedy this. It has been remarkable that education is available to the vast majority of our children. But what about the quality of the majority of our graduates, and especially those students who leave school after Sijil Rendah Pelajaran (SRP). Though literate, they are not really ready for the employment market.

It would be useful if all those who drop out of our school system after SRP are sent to technical and trade schools where they can acquire useful skills. At present they are not adequately equipped to be really useful in manufacturing or in the service industries. These sectors require a higher order of knowledge and skills. So the large number of dropouts settle for low-productivity and low-income jobs. This is a waste of good human resources and a loss to the economy.

Just as importantly, we will need to give higher recognition to our teaching profession at all levels. Teachers and lecturers have gradually lost out to their counterparts in other professions in terms of salaries and social status. Consequently, we may not be attracting or retaining enough good quality human resources in the teaching profession. This can have adverse effects on the quality of teaching and the quality of our graduates from the Malaysian education system. The Minister of Education, Dato' Sri Mohd Najib Tun Abdul Razak Hussein has been trying hard to improve the career prospects of teachers, but more needs to be done by the Government.

Unless the quality of our teachers improve with better prospects, their morale will suffer and our education standards will decline. Then our 7th Malaysia Plan objectives to raise efficiency and productivity will be compromised. But the improvement of quality and productivity does not depend solely on our education system. Quality upgrading should take place right through life. For this, the government and the private sector must spend much more on training, especially at the workplace. The government's plan to introduce Total Quality Management (TQM) and ISO 9000 will help to improve efficiency in the government's machinery, but it must be given higher priority.

Similarly, the private sector too should step up its training programmes and increase its research and development. At present, the private sector is seriously lagging behind in R&D. How then can the private sector compete internationally in the longer term if it does so little for training and research and development. Unfortunately, most companies are profit-oriented in the short term and do not fully appreciate the rich rewards of training in the longer term.

Modifying the NDP

But in the final analysis, Malaysians must change their mind-sets. We have to revise our policies and our attitudes, if we are to become more output- and productivity-oriented as envisaged in the 7th Malaysia Plan. This will call for more competition, less protection and reduced preferential treatment. It will mean the reduction of the rentier class, which includes all those who get preferences for licences and government contracts. This will be difficult to do expeditiously but it has to be done if we are to develop greater competitiveness and more efficiency in our economic system. This means that we must strongly but steadily and steadfastly modify our National Development Policy to become more competitive and to sustain our socio-economic success.

After all, the major concerns that brought about the NEP and then the NDP have been largely overcome. Poverty eradication in 1996 is no longer the burning issue that it was in 1969. There is also the promise and the prospect that poverty will be very minimal in the next few years, except for hard-core and structural poverty, which is still prevalent even in the United States.

Furthermore, the second prong of the NEP has also achieved much success. The pillars of the Malaysian economy, i.e. banking, insurance, shipping, electricity, telecommunications, etc. are largely owned by the Bumiputeras or the Government itself. So the 20 per cent Bumiputera share of the corporate sector is really much larger in terms of "real" ownership.

Thus, I believe that the original objectives of the NEP and now the NDP have been significantly achieved. It is therefore now reasonable to be more relaxed in the implementation of these socio-economic national policies, with a view to realising greater national unity and competitiveness. That way we will be able to became more open and ready to take on foreign competition more successfully and to participate more actively in the international arena.

The Challenge

I believe the 7th Malaysia Plan is highly commendable in seeking to achieve higher productivity in the use of our God-given resources. But a plan is merely a document, a blueprint. We will have to effectively implement the 7th Malaysia Plan, if its laudable objectives are to be realised.

We are fortunate in having strong and visionary leaders to ensure the plan's success. We must lay firm foundations for the 21st century. We must not fail posterity.

However, I am convinced that God willing, we will succeed to give every Malaysian a progressive place under the Malaysian sun. We must slowly move towards giving more equal opportunities to all Malaysians to compete on equal terms. Only then will we be able to maximise productivity and our national potential. That would be a challenge for the nation and our leaders.

12.

PROPOSALS FOR
IMPROVEMENT OF PLAN

THE main thrust of the 7th Malaysia Plan is the accelerated promotion of productivity. Higher productivity will enhance economic growth even without significantly increasing all the factors of production like land, labour, capital and entrepreneurial skills. Productivity- or output-driven economic growth will achieve sustainable balance of payments and price stability as well. But more has to be done to improve implementation.

Investment- or input-driven growth may not be sustainable in the longer term. It could also lead to larger balance of payments deficits and price instability because of the relatively inefficient use of resources. This phenomenon has occurred in the Malaysian economy over the years, as evidenced by the high Incremental Capital Output Ratio. This means that for every ringgit that we invest, the value of the output is less than one ringgit.

The 7th Malaysia Plan is therefore commendable in recognising the underlying weaknesses in the Malaysian economy that need to be reduced, if not removed, if our growth is to be sustained.

However, the 7th Malaysia Plan itself does not adequately include the specific policies and especially the detailed programmes that have to be implemented to realise the objectives of increasing the Total Factor Productivity in the economy. Since it is only a Plan, it postulates policies and targets but not detailed programmes.

Total Factor Productivity can only be improved if workers are made more productive, and the techniques of production and work processes are made more efficient. For all these, we need to select the right person for the job. We cannot afford to be partial and paternalistic.

The Annual Budgets will therefore need to have specific programmes to raise Total Factor Productivity. Increased productivity cannot be attained in a few Budgets, but has to be realised over the longer term, on a consistent and continuous basis. Increasing the TFP is actually raising the efficiency of human resources and systems. This cannot be done on an *ad-hoc* or piecemeal basis. Raising the TFP cannot be handled superficially; it has to be approached as a paradigm shift and must involve radical changes. It would mean even modifying the National Development Policy.

In view of these considerations, the following proposals are made to promote productivity-driven growth in the short term.

Short-term Proposals to Improve Productivity

Training of Workers. In the short term, emphasis should be placed on training workers and upgrading their skills. Approved training programmes should be given more attractive tax reliefs. Grants based on a ringgit-for-ringgit or a similar basis should be given to the business sector to encourage more in-house training.

Training institutes for skilled workers should be encouraged to be established by the private sector. According to the 7th Malaysia Plan, the intake of skilled and semi-skilled manpower by local public training institutions is expected to rise by only 6.1 per cent by 2000, over the 43,100 in 1995. This is unimpressive considering Malaysia's vast national demand for skilled workers.

In 1995, there were 65 private skills training institutions that produced 8,300 graduates in mechanical, civil and computer engineering and information technology. There is certainly much greater scope here for the government to provide more incentives to increase this small output many times over.

During the 6th Malaysia Plan period, only 3,200 workers were produced from the evening classes in technical subjects held at government educational institutions. These institutions are grossly under-utilised and the Treasury should make it more attractive for the private sector to increase the output of this category of trainees.

The Human Resource Development Fund expended only RM140 million since 1993 to train 639,000 industrial workers. The Government would need to examine why more was not spent on this important training programme and why it is necessary to restrict this scheme only to companies with a paid-up capital of more than RM2.5 million. We need to be more liberal if we are to be more effective in utilising the Human Resource Development Fund. The need for training is greatest for the smaller firms, where the paid-up capital is less than RM2.5 million. So where is the priority?

Transfer of Technology. Advanced skills training that is provided by foreign governments is minimal. The German programme produced only 57 graduates in 1995, the Malaysian French Institute has a capacity of only about 600 trainees, while the Japan-Malaysia Technical Institute is still in its planning stage. These countries and others have benefited so much from investments in Malaysia, but may have not transferred sufficient technology to us. They should be urged to do much more training. If they need tax incentives, the Government should consider their requests seriously. The United States, the United Kingdom, Russia and Singapore, *inter alia*, should be encouraged to set up similar institutes, to expand advanced skills training which is in severe short supply. This would encourage healthy competition among these donor countries.

The transfer of technology and training in multinational corporations should be monitored. If they are found to be non-cooperative, they should be penalised by a reduction in tax relief. In other words, multinationals that do not invest enough in training should be discouraged from further government concessions. They need not be encouraged to expand their investment. Instead, the more co-operative and empathetic foreign investors could be encouraged to invest more in the country.

Policy Changes. Distance learning should also be further encouraged. With Internet now readily available, we should expand the opportunities to upgrade skills and knowledge, especially among those who have not had the benefit of formal education. More opportunities should be given to those who have been denied educational access, regardless of ethnicity.

Malay, the national language, will have to be strengthened further especially to consolidate our national identity and unity. But the English language will have to be promoted more effectively to increase productivity. The ability to communicate well in English will allow us to absorb knowledge and increase our role in global competition in most fields.

Labour-intensive industries will need to be scaled down by phasing out the many incentives and tax concessions that labour-intensive industries now enjoy. The Budgets will have to show that the Government is serious about moving out of labour-intensive industries by further raising incentives for more capital-intensive and high-technology industries.

Research and Development. Technology, and research and development need to be considerably expanded. The private sector has been slow to undertake research and development. The R&D incentives have to be reviewed and made more attractive. One way of encouraging more R&D would be to give grants on the basis of some formula, like ringgit for ringgit, for research and also skill training and development. Another way is to commercialise R&D through the syndication of R&D, on a case-by-case basis.

The Flexi Wage System has been talked about for a long time but has not really taken off. The government must lead in implementing the Flexi Wage System through some incentive schemes, if necessary. Both employers and employees could be provided tax incentives, initially at least, to adopt the Flexi Wage System.

The Annual Budgets must ensure the efficient utilisation of capital even though raising funds locally has been relatively easy.

As capital is scarce, the Budgets must continue to encourage savings by giving tax incentives and keeping interest rates attractive enough for

90

longer term savings. Interest rates need to be higher than the inflation rates to sustain the confidence to increase savings.

Long-term Proposals to Overcome Productivity Constraints

We have discussed some of the short-term proposals to enhance productivity. But we have to address the longer-term issues and proposals as well because they are more difficult and structural in nature. Unless these fundamental issues are tackled, our efforts to enhance productivity in the longer term will be seriously constrained.

Inter-ethnic and Intra-ethnic Competition. The drive to increase productivity has its limitations in Malaysia. The Malaysian Prime Minister, Dato Seri Dr Mahathir Mohamad, has said that Malaysia's policy does not envisage full and open competition in our society, given the fact that some ethnic groups are not ready at this stage of our socio-economic development. What we have in Malaysia is intra-ethnic competition and not inter-ethnic and general competition. It is supposed to be like golf where golfers with different handicaps play with each other, rather than against each other. Each player's performance is measured against his own standard and not against the standard of other players who may have lower handicaps. That is why we cannot be entirely efficiency-oriented, at least for the time being.

This arrangement has worked well and has brought about stability, security and continued prosperity for the country. However, we must now find ways to reduce intra-ethnic income disparity in order to increase overall competition. The privileged and better qualified who are protected against inter-ethnic competition have benefited considerably and even disproportionately, if measured against their talents and efforts. These protected and privileged individuals and companies may not learn the real lessons of genuine market competition and thus may not be able to adequately cope with competition in the global market. Thus they would not be able to value-add or expand their business or make it more profitable in the longer term. If this happens, our privileged businessmen would not be contributing to our national competitiveness.

They would not be able to lead in business and lead our country to greater heights in international trade and investment.

Of course, there are some outstanding exceptions. But exceptions do not make the rule. In general, therefore, we will need to give preferences more and more on the basis of merit and not other considerations. If we continue to encourage nepotism, privileges and preferences, then the net result is that Malaysia as a whole will lose out in international competitiveness. Our exports could decline. Our service industries such as shipping, freight, insurance, banking, professional services, consultancy and trading, could be adversely affected. The situation could be further aggravated with the opening up of the economy as demanded by the World Trade Organisation.

Loss of Competitiveness

The immediate consequence of a drop in our competitiveness is that our balance of payments would become strained. If unchecked through enhanced competition and higher exports of goods and services, then the economy itself could weaken. Our impressive economic growth could slow down. Lower rates of economic growth would mean lower incomes and possibly less employment opportunities. We have taken high growth, high employment and low inflation for granted. Our continuing success could make us over-confident and complacent, and could lull us into a false sense of security. We may think "lets enjoy the good life while we can. We do not have to work too hard to sustain the good life." Such a mind-set would be dangerous.

Any slowdown in the economy will cause hardship to the lower income groups, particularly those who will become unemployed. Thus, the policies aimed at creating a wealthy upper-middle class could cause the poor to suffer. If this happens, then it will be a case of "reverse subsidy", where the poorer people will be subsidising the privileged and making them richer.

But how do we create an intra-ethnic wealthy class without adversely affecting the poorer classes? How do we help some of the promising professionals and businessmen to become rich without hurting the others? One clear way to help individuals become millionaires while not giving them too many business opportunities too soon is by not "spoiling" them. The new generation of businessmen should be encouraged to compete in the marketplace and to work their way up the ladder. They should not be given too much preference. It is counter productive and inimical to their long-term development.

Spread Privileges

Moreover, it is better to give a wider selection of businessmen the opportunities to undertake large contracts and be awarded privileged licenses, than to confine these privileges to a select few. It is more equitable to spread the giving of privileges to more businessmen. After all, not all beneficiaries will succeed. Many will fail. Even those who succeed may not be successful for long, unless they have learnt how to compete. But how can they compete effectively if they have not been given the chance to compete? They must be given time to build good track records in order to compete efficiently. We should thus provide privileges in small doses. Those who get large concessions and privileges usually pay large salaries to professional managers and just sit back and enjoy the profits.

The new Government-nominated entrepreneurs will not be in a strong position to inspire enterprise and leadership among their managers because they may not have much or even show much enterprise and leadership themselves. Consequently, we may not develop world-class companies. We may not even be able to compete with businessmen and companies in our neighbouring countries and the region. It may be more productive to allow more management buyouts (MBOs) of privatised government agencies and statutory bodies.

No one individual need control more than 50 per cent of the equity shares of a company. The ownership could be spread out more equitably. The top managers could of course be given higher vested interests in the companies. Then we will have the best of both worlds. The professional managers will have a strong vested interest in the company. At the same time, they will not be allowed to become mere paid employees who may not be sufficiently motivated. Furthermore, this arrangement will reduce the risk of having one uncompetitive majority shareholder who could lead the company down the drain, especially if he is relatively inexperienced. In this case, not only the company and its shareholders will lose out but the whole economy will be affected. Our entrepreneurs, therefore, need to be genuine, tough, competitive, innovative and sustained in their efforts to succeed. Only then will they become real assets to the country and society. Otherwise, they will be liabilities in the future. Then we will all suffer for their failures. We need winners and not losers to drive our economy towards Vision 2020.

National Competitive Policy: More Equal Opportunities

It is recognised that intra-ethnic competition will need to continue in order to sustain and increase national unity and stability. But we will need to plan from now to work harder towards relatively increased and wider competition within the whole economy. Otherwise, Malaysia as a whole will lose out to other countries. We will need to modify the National Development Policy, especially in view of the onslaught of new policies set by the new WTO. We will perhaps need a new National Competitive Policy that will prepare all communities to compete more openly and as early as possible.

By the year 2000, Malaysia could concentrate more on providing equal opportunities for education, especially to the underprivileged groups, regardless of race. Once they have been trained and qualified, then we should allow the graduates to compete openly and equally to increase their competitive position in the world. Too much protection for too long can be inhibitive and inimical to the competitive spirit. It will constrain the promotion of productivity-driven and sustained socioeconomic growth and undermine Malaysia's economic progress. We will need to decide soon when we can start preparing for the new era of global competition with a new National Competitive Policy.

Rewarding Science Graduates

National competitiveness will also be considerably raised if we are able to give much higher rewards to our graduates in science and technology at all levels. Students should be encouraged to take science studies seriously from the primary level onwards. More scholarships should be awarded for science and technological studies. More scholarships should be given to science scholars rather than those in the liberal arts, law and business studies. After all, if liberal arts graduates are paid higher or have better career prospects than their science and engineering counterparts, then we will continue to be technologically uncompetitive and short of scientific manpower.

The education system should be changed to encourage Arts students to take science subjects and science students to have a better appreciation of language and literature. In this way, graduates of either stream will be able to fit into the scientific society of tomorrow. They will be able to adapt better to rapid technological change.

Revise Salary Structure

More importantly, our whole salary structure should be changed. At present, liberal arts graduates have much better career prospects than science and engineering graduates. Consequently, the incentives for a good science student to take up a scientific, technological or engineering course are poor. That is why most students shun science subjects at school. Why should they struggle with mathematics and the sciences which are generally regarded as tougher and harder courses compared to softer choices like history, geography, literature and accounting. Furthermore, why should they have to work so hard on science and maths courses when in the end their peers who graduate as business, communications, marketing, accounts and law graduates earn much better even earlier in their careers.

The highest-paid officials in the government service are arts graduates in the Malaysian Administrative and Diplomatic Services. Engineers, scientists and teachers are paid much less. Furthermore, the career prospects of the Administrators and Diplomats are far superior. The ratios of promotion to superscale posts are more favourable for the Administrators and Diplomats than all the professional and technical services.

95

So why should students opt for science degrees when arts degrees give them an easier time at school and college and a more rewarding working life? This kind of thinking and value system for students is understandable. However, it is not beneficial for the country's future and its march towards a more competitive and industrial society. Vision 2020 will be jeopardised unless the Government acts now to elevate the status of science and technology at schools and universities. Science teachers and university lecturers should be paid more. Engineers and other scientific staff should be given better salaries and career prospects. Only then will they be able to produce a science-and-technology-based society. Otherwise, we will continue to erode our competitiveness as we move rapidly into a more competitive global village.

Productivity and Sustained Growth
There is a strong relationship between increasing productivity and attaining sustainable equilibrium in the balance of payments and price stability and long-term growth. Higher productivity implies enhanced efficiency in the use of resources. Greater efficiency leads to increased competitiveness. Thus, not only is the production of goods and services increased, but their quality will improve. More and better output leads to more exports, relatively less dependence on imports and, therefore, a stronger balance of payments and stronger socio-economic growth. Similarly, more output in food and other goods and services will help to lower prices. Price stability is thus more likely to be sustained with more efficient production rather than price controls.

Productivity-driven economic growth also helps to attain more balanced growth. Our scarce resources will then be utilised more efficiently and therefore conserved more rationally. Thus, our land, timber, minerals, oil and gas resources will not be exploited carelessly but on a more sustainable basis. Our environment will be better protected.

Conclusion
In the final analysis, only higher productivity will ensure sustained economic growth and stability. There is a limit to the exploitation of our re-

sources. But there is greater potential to expand the limits of human resources, ingenuity and productivity, together with technology.

Thus Malaysia will have to concentrate more on developing our human resources. However, human resources can only be fully developed in an environment of free and open competition, to stretch the limits of human potential. Thus the National Development Policy will need to be reviewed and revised and a new National Competitive Policy introduced soon to enable Malaysia to effectively meet the challenges of the 21st century and to attain the objectives of Vision 2020 on time.

PART THREE
THE CIVIL SERVICE

13.

PROFESSIONALS
IN THE CIVIL SERVICE

THE public service has to be reformed if it is to meet and deliver the challenges of Vision 2020. This chapter deals with the professionals and the larger number of employees at the lower levels of public service.

The Professional Services

Professionals like teachers, lawyers, doctors and engineers should be granted all the favourable considerations given to the Pegawai Tadbiran dan Diplomatik (PTD) and perhaps even more, since the professionals are a rarer breed. The existing disincentives should be removed and incentives increased for professional officers. The following issues need to be addressed on a priority basis to improve the professional services in the government sector, if we are to see more efficiency and get more value out of taxpayers' money.

First, professionals should not be treated inferior to the PTD, i.e. the top civil servants and diplomats. They should be given more opportunities for promotion to superscale posts. Presently, the ratio of superscale posts to the timescale posts is much more favourable for the administrative and diplomatic officers. Though the ratios have improved greatly over the years, the professionals in government service still feel relatively shortchanged with regard to promotion opportunities compared with their administrative counterparts.

Second, professionals should be allowed more time to practise their professions without having to do much administrative work. This work could be better undertaken by the less technical administrative types.

However, the professionals tend to want to move into administrative positions mainly because their promotion prospects in their respective professions are restricted or suppressed by administrative officers of the PTD, as claimed by the professionals.

There is some basis for this allegation, since the Public Service Department and the Budget Division of the Treasury, which decide on creating superscale posts, are staffed entirely by the PTD, i.e. the Administrative Officers.

The professionals generally believe they are therefore not treated fairly in their careers. That is why there is a serious shortage of professionals in the government service.

Third, professionals could be allowed to earn part-time income after office hours, if they so desire. This arrangement can narrow the income gap between those in the government sector and that of their better-paid counterparts in the private sector.

Private practice can be allowed since most professionals are not generally involved in sensitive national policy formulation, unlike the PTD. Although there could be some conflict of interest, I am sure we can find ways and means to minimise any abuse. We should not "oppose" a good scheme that could be beneficial to many, just because it could be abused by a few. This part-time private practice could apply especially to doctors and teachers. The approvals could be discretionary, depending on their work performance.

Fourth, professionals should be given better equipment. They often complain that their office facilities are unsuitable and inferior compared to those provided for the PTD.

Teachers often do not even have decent classrooms and common rooms. Doctors complain that the top superscale officers do not have secretaries to answer phone calls and to provide simple support services.

Consequently, they feel very discriminated and frustrated. It is not only the higher pay in the private sector that matters; it is the feeling that they are being bullied and pushed around by the PTD and even the administrative staff at the lower levels!

If professional officers are treated on par with the senior PTD officers, there would be less frustration and feelings of being like *anak angkat* or stepchildren. We have to rectify the situation. Consult the professionals and they will tell us how to do it. They are not asking for much.

Fifth, promotions of professionals, and indeed those in the service, should be based on performance and less on ethnic considerations. Promotions not based on performance constitute the surest way to reduce morale, initiative and overall efficiency and commitment to serve the government and people. This is one of the major reasons why there are so many frustrated professionals. This frustration also explains why so many are leaving the government service. Each promotion provides only a few hundred dollars, so why deny the professionals more and fairer promotions?

Seventh, practically all Secretaries-General of ministries and Directors-General of professional departments are Bumiputeras. Why must senior positions be so exclusive? This is a mind-set that will need to change soon. In the past, the private sector was quite exclusively dominated by non-Bumiputeras. It's a different scenario today. Many of the most important and strategic corporations are headed and run by Bumiputeras. So there should be more balance in the public sector as there is now in the private sector. The Civil Service must become more reflective of the society it serves.

The General Civil Service

The general civil service is made up of executives, clerks, typists, technicians and some lower grade workers. Most of them would qualify for membership in the Congress of Unions of Employees in the Public and Civil Services (Cuepacs). This is the group that has spearheaded the fight for higher wages. This is the group that will get the bulk of the RM3 billion from the new salary revision and bonus. This is also the group where the quality of performance and productivity are relatively lower compared to the private sector. This may be because of the low pay, the lack of incentives and also the lack of motivation. Consequently, the Government could be attracting lower-quality staff to serve the people!

This is where the poor quality shows up: inefficient counter services to the public. This is where the public feel let down by the civil service.

Some will argue that the civil servants are neither civil nor are they service-oriented. But this is where there is the greatest need to improve the public service and indeed the government's image. There is so much of *tidak apa* attitude, indifference and rudeness at the lower levels of the civil service. The public see this everyday and it is bad for the government.

The government should therefore take more serious steps to improve the quality of the civil service, otherwise there could be a decline in public confidence.

What can be done to improve the efficiency of the lower-grade workers in the public service?

First, the labour intensive nature of work must be converted to more modern technological methods. There should be more office automation. The use of computers should be stepped up to reduce the slow and outdated systems and procedures. Office systems and procedures have to be modernised. We should not be told that it is difficult to locate files or that they have been lost. Administrative delays breed corruption and more inefficiency.

Second, the large number of employees recruited under the unfortunate *Isi Penuh* campaign a few years ago should be radically reduced. We should not have quantity to substitute for poor quality staff. We need not have two or more staff to do the job of one person, if the standards of recruitment and performance are higher. We do not want a bloated public service that is also not so efficient.

Third, the government should attract the best and not the least qualified or the poorest calibre staff. If the SPM grade is the minimum qualification for entry into the clerical service, then only those with the better grades should be recruited. The government should not be in the position of having to scrape the barrel to recruit its staff. Weak staff provide poor back-up services and dismal counter services.

Fourth, teachers and lecturers who form the bulk of government employees need to be given better training opportunities so that they can be emplaced at higher levels of government service. Their entry qualifications could be raised and training enhanced so that the future generations of the workforce will be better qualified.

We cannot aspire to produce an efficient workforce for Vision 2020 if our teachers are poorly qualified, inadequately paid and demoralised. Their salary structure and career prospects need to be improved. They should be allowed to do more teaching and be relieved of minor administrative chores, which undermine their ambition to be good professional teachers and lecturers.

Fifth, discipline among civil servants should be strongly emphasised. There should be no political or ethnic considerations in enforcing disciplinary standards. At present there is too much laxity as shown by long coffee breaks, lethargy and indifference of the staff manning the service counters and, worse still, even among the lower-rank staff in Government hospitals.

Sixth, privatisation needs to be speeded up to introduce greater competition and customer orientation in the civil service. However, privatisation should not be preoccupied with just raising fees and cutting corners in order to reward employees. Salary increases should be commensurate with increase in productivity. I wish Cuepacs will spend some time organising courses, with the government's help, on how to raise productivity and dedication, instead of being preoccupied in clamouring for higher wages. Cuepacs could get more involved in TQM training.

Seventh, a more multiracial civil service will make it easier for the government to deliver the goods, even during major festive seasons when employees take their leave. It is most disconcerting to see practically empty offices on some festive periods. We are not a homogeneous society where all our people celebrate the same festivals. Worse still, there are some staff who take leave for every festival. This bad practice has got to stop if we are to be more efficient. We cannot be allowed to have the best of all worlds.

Moreover, a multiracial public service encourages healthy competition. It will reduce the negative effects of in-breeding, paternalism and nepotism.

New Remuneration Scheme

Finally, I would again appeal to the powers that be to refine and improve the New Remuneration Scheme (NRS). If it is causing so much heartache and frustration, we should seriously try to modify it. Perhaps we should reward the good performers with better bonuses and smaller increments, rather than give them large jumps in increments that could encourage complacency amongst those promoted rapidly.

The present NRS or "Skim Saraan Baru" is treated with little respect if most public servants resentfully call it "Saya Sayang Boss"! The public servants can be given all the hardware, software, performance targets, charters, guidelines and encouragements. But if they are not motivated by high ideals and satisfactory rewards, the public service will not respond effectively to our national aspirations.

Unless the whole public service is reviewed, revamped and reformed, it will be more difficult to achieve the grand socio-economic objectives of Vision 2020. This should be a major policy priority of the government. We need to move faster or we will be left behind in the global race towards the 21st century.

Serious Mistake

Finally, it is of vital national interest that the Government recruits and maintains a large or fair share of Malaysia's best brains in the public service. We could be making a serious mistake if we do not attract some of the best brains in the country. In time the Government machinery could weaken. Political leaders then will not have the benefit of sound professional advice. The business community will then exert inordinate influence on Ministers and State Government political leaders. This would not be good for the nation in the longer term.

To attain higher standards, the Government would therefore need to give much higher priority to reforming the public service by making it more efficient and by providing better salaries and conditions of service.

14.

COMPENSATING
THE CIVIL SERVICE

THE government has decided to increase the salary bill for its 850,000 civil servants by about RM2 billion. Another RM1 billion will be given out as bonus for 1995. This is fine for the civil servants who deserve it, but the public asks whether it is fair to pay so much to so many civil servants. This total sum of RM3 billion will probably recur every year, assuming the economy continues to do well and an annual bonus of RM1 billion is given out every year. This means the government's budget on its current account will show a smaller surplus by an additional RM3 billion every year.

But it is not a question of whether the government's budget can bear this burden. Rather, the question is, could the government have saved this RM3 billion. The answer is no. We cannot afford to underpay civil servants and yet expect high performance from them. It is neither fair nor reasonable.

Is it worth it?

The public service salaries like their counterparts in the private sector had to be raised to keep up with at least the rising prices as well as to narrow the widening wage gap with salaries in the private sector. The wages have been particularly low amongst the lower levels of the public service, who find it difficult to make ends meet even for the most basic goods and services. I believe that the increased wage bill is therefore fair and justified.

But the public still asks whether the salary revision will benefit the people?

It is difficult to say for sure. If the salaries were not raised, morale and productivity would have fallen further. However, now that salaries have been raised, we are not sure that productivity will rise. The public cannot be sure that the efficiency of the public service, particularly at the lower echelons and at the levels of the public counter services, will improve. This is the concern of the public. People do not mind giving civil servants a better deal, but will the civil servants give the public their money's worth? Will the civil servants just take the higher salaries and still continue to give relatively poor services to the public?

Prime Minister Dato Seri Dr Mahathir Mohamad and the former Chief Secretary to the Government Tan Sri Ahmad Sarji Abdul Hamid have done a great deal to exhort the public service to be more efficient. All this undoubtedly helped in improving the quality and standard of the civil service to some extent. But these improvements have not been enough to meet the dynamic challenges and changes taking place internationally and at home. I believe that the world, our own leaders and indeed our country, are all moving faster than our civil service can cope with. Our public service at the lower and middle levels are lagging behind. They could be our Achilles' heel in our race to achieve Vision 2020.

What is required is a review and reform of the whole public service for it to really improve to match our aspirations and expectations for Vision 2020. And in the meantime, what can we do to improve the public service?

Review the NRS

The first priority would be to review the New Remuneration Scheme (NRS) and to improve it where necessary. The NRS is a laudable effort at initial reform. However, much of its rough edges have to be removed. The NRS has to be kept, but it has to be refined to improve the morale and efficiency of the whole public service. Otherwise the NRS will remain unpopular and even be resented and the morale of the public service will remain low.

There are many cases of senior and less senior officers and staff earning the same salary because they are in the same salary band. Surely, there must be different salaries for different levels of seniority for those in the same grade. Otherwise respect for seniors will decline and lead to the breakdown in discipline.

The NRS aims to promote productivity but it will need to be improved to attain greater productivity in the public service. We need the NRS but we also need to remove its anomalies. Then the public service will support the NRS strongly and be happy about it. So my appeal to the powers-that-be is to improve the NRS and make it more acceptable to the whole public service.

Reform Administrative Service

The government could also reform the apex of the administration which is the administrative and diplomatic services (PTD). It could be reformed along the following lines.

First, the entry qualifications should be more stringent and recruitment should be much more competitive. The quality of recruits into the public service must be as good as those of top corporations.

Second, the entry salaries and career prospects should be comparable to those in the private sector, although it will be difficult to place it on par. It is said that if we pay the least we will get the worst.

Third, more candidates should be drawn from the scientific disciplines and less from the arts, to fit into the mould of a science-oriented society. The higher echelons of the public service are now mostly liberal arts graduates who need not be the best of all our graduates.

Fourth, promotions should be more rapid and worthwhile. It is demoralising to wait for several years to move up grades, only to get small salary increases. There are thousands of cases of bright, hard-working civil servants who have been stuck for years on the same grades or who have reached their maximum salaries. When they reach a dead end, we force them to become deadwood!

Fifth, housing loans should be made more attractive to encourage more house ownership. Housing is a major expenditure item in the budget of all salaried workers. It is a more significant proportion in the civil servants' budget, only because the salaries are generally lower than those in the private sector. It would help greatly to increase the morale of the civil service, raise its productivity and enhance its commitment and loyalty, if only more is done to enable wider house ownership. State governments can be pushed to provide more suitable land for government housing for civil servants.

Similarly, student loan schemes should also be made more easily available to the civil servants' children who qualify to enter institutions of higher learning. The biggest setback for civil servants are the inability and the frustration of not being able to send their children for higher education. A subsidised student loan fund should be set up to enable bright children of civil servants to go for higher education.

Sixth, more opportunities should be provided to civil servants to train at home and abroad at universities to enhance professionalism. Remedial courses in the English language could be given to ensure that our civil servants can be admitted to the best universities in the world. They have to be equipped to compete with the civil servants and diplomats from foreign countries.

Seventh, attract and retain graduates with the right values and dedication to serve God, King and Country. The civil servant will increasingly have to be someone who is committed to serve his fellow countrymen, without too much regard for monetary rewards. The recruitment process will have to reject those candidates who are mercenary. Money should not be the motive for joining the public service.

Eighth, provide better physical and technological facilities and more pleasant working environments. This will inspire a sense of professionalism, enhance performance and promote a stronger sense of well-being. Indeed, it is unfair to expect civil servants to perform well when he is not given good office equipment like personal computers, modern telecommunication facilities and even comfortable furniture.

Ninth, the PTD should reduce its in-breeding by becoming more multiracial and more reflective of the society it serves. More internal competition and sharing of the positive values of all the ethnic groups in Malaysia will help build national unity and efficiency. How can any society increase its confidence in its civil service if it is dominated by one ethnic group. How can we ensure proper discipline when civil servants who insist on discipline are easily misconstrued as being insensitive.

Tenth, the government could give more public recognition and self-respect to the civil service for its invaluable service to the nation. In 1996, not even one civil servant was bestowed with a *Tan Sri*-ship! It must be remembered that without the civil service's contribution, the government cannot function and business cannot prosper. But does the public realise this simple truth?

Many believe it is the political leaders alone who do the hard thinking and the hard work. But our political leaders know better. Without the dedicated efforts of our top civil servants and professionals, our political leaders will not be able to deliver effectively to the nation. Fortunately, with the help of our top civil servants and professionals, they have been able to do so thus far.

Finally, unless the elite PTD or the backbone of the public service, as the Prime Minister has described the PTD, is reformed and made more quality-oriented, the government machinery to deliver Vision 2020 will weaken.

We have to reform and refine our civil service now to ensure the realisation of Vision 2020.

15.

RAISING EFFICIENCY

OVER the years, Malaysia's policies and performance at home and abroad have raised the self-respect of Malaysians and we have also earned the respect of foreigners.

Our Prime Minister has always stressed the importance of earning national self-respect and national pride. He has said, "We want the country to be respected. We don't want people to look down upon us. The only way we can do that, the only way we can have people show us respect is by being able to achieve and if possible outdo other people". This quotation is taken from his speech to Malaysian students at Cambridge University recently.

But what is the real situation at home? While there is no doubt that we have come a long way towards improving our national efficiency since *Merdeka*, we still have a long way to go. In fact, the Government's frequent exhortation to become more efficient have caused us to realise more painfully that the gap between expectations and the reality in achieving higher efficiency, is still wide.

Inefficiencies
There is a long agenda of areas of inadequate efficiency that have to be addressed.

First, the widening gap between faster wage increases and a slower rise in productivity gives a broad indicator of this slower pace in the rate of increase in our national efficiency. We could do much more to increase training on the job, revise our education system and expand tertiary education and research and development.

The Government is now also in a better position to introduce the Flexi Wage System. The Government has a broader responsibility to the nation as a whole, unlike trade union leaders who are required to look at the vested interests of their supporters for survival.

The Government therefore has to act more purposefully to promote a productivity-related wage system that has to be efficient and just to both unions management and workers for the progress of the whole nation.

Second, our Incremental Capital Output Ratio is relatively high. This means that for every ringgit of capital investment, the return in output has been relatively low. That is to say that the way we use our capital has not been as efficient as it could be. We have been able to get away with it, because Malaysia has not had serious problems with attracting capital from abroad. Furthermore, our national savings rate at about 30 per cent per annum has been high and so we now do not have to borrow much.

But imagine how much more we would have achieved, how much less capital would have been used and how much better our collective quality of life would have been, if we had been more efficient than we already are, not only with our spending, but in so many other respects.

Third, let's take the case of our food production. Food contributes about 34 per cent of our basket of goods and services that are used for compiling our Consumer Price Index. If food production were higher then more food supplies would be available. Thus the costs of food like fish, meat, vegetables and fruit would be less expensive. Instead of rising by 5 per cent to 12 per cent per annum for different food items, we could be paying far less for these basic food items and the cost of living would be lower. Food prices keep rising mainly because of some inefficiencies, which fortunately are being removed with more liberal policies.

Fourth, we have major problems in obtaining suitable farming land. Land Offices have generally not been efficient in alienating land expeditiously. This has discouraged food production, especially on a large scale commercial basis. Similarly, fish is expensive because the cold storage facilities are inadequate and so fish catches get spoilt. There is therefore, considerable wastage. Financial resources could be more efficiently allocated and utilised in the agricultural sector, to increase food production to reduce food prices.

Fifth, we have to reiterate the serious constraints in obtaining suitable land for low-cost housing. Indeed the system of land allocation and especially, the many procedural hurdles that have to be crossed in obtaining so many approvals for building houses, compound inefficiencies in the whole system. Computerisation is now being introduced at Land Offices. This is helpful. However, introduction is one thing while full-scale implementation of the computerisation is something else.

Sixth, our transportation system could be made more efficient to get food supplies from the farms to the consumers. Although the road systems have definitely improved, the efficiency of road haulage leaves much to be desired. All these deficiencies and inefficiencies in the transportation system add to the costs of supplying food in the towns.

Seventh, the inefficient urban transport system is causing much loss in time, energy and investment opportunities. Although there are many transportation projects now in place, it is still uncertain as to whether they will be efficient enough to solve the present traffic nightmares. It begs the question as to why we had to wait to get to this stage of inefficiency in public transport, haulage and port management. It is hoped that we will give more priority to forward planning and financial allocations for transport in the future.

One key transport mode that needs greater attention is our bus and taxi system. It is not understood why it is taking so long to amalgamate the twelve bus companies in and around Kuala Lumpur. Why are we so soft on big bus companies at the expense of the thousands of school children, low income office workers and public who are constantly bullied by reckless and ruthless big bus drivers. Is it fair? Our taxis too leave much to be desired. They often do not stop for you, overcharge you and are often terribly rude. It does not cost more money but only requires better organisation and a will to initiate new policies to have a more efficient bus and taxi systems.

Eighth, our enforcement could be made much more efficient. There is no need to keep introducing new laws when the existing laws are not effectively enforced. The rising tragedies and fatalities on our roads could be reduced, if traffic laws are enforced more stringently and punitively. When thousands of summons can be ignored for so long, something must be really wrong. Garbage continues to be indiscriminately littered in our parks, rivers and housing estates. Even deadly cyanide and toxic wastes are carelessly handled because of inadequate co-ordination among our agencies and the consequential slack enforcement.

Ninth, the long queues at our National Registration Departments and some other Departments could be significantly reduced. Surely, we can spare our people the hassle of going round in circles to get good service which is after all their legitimate right. The Inland Revenue Department has shown much initiative by going out to the people. But is it only because money is to be collected? However, dealing with the IRD is still time-consuming. Could not other departments provide similar meet-the-people services?

It is a poor reflection on the administration when basic services become difficult to get efficiently. Our people must be extremely tolerant to take poor Government services for granted. But the Government should not tolerate inefficient public services nor take the people's patience for granted. As I have stated before, it is the counter services that bring discredit to the Government. Why is the Government tolerating what is working against its good image?

The Public Complaints Bureau could highlight the major weaknesses which could then be given priority for improvement. What is often lacking is proper supervision, inadequate computer facilities and poorly qualified and badly trained staff on the ground.

Tenth, I've maintained that the Government pensioners have got a raw deal because of some careless planning and indifference to the concept of a caring society. Previously, they would get their Pension Vouchers which could be cashed or deposited in any bank. Suddenly, however, this facility was withdrawn and pensioners are now required to open bank accounts only in the two largest Government-owned banks, i.e. Malayan Banking and Bank Bumiputera Malaysia, and in Bank Simpanan Nasional. These three institutions do not have as many branches as all the other financial institutions put together. So, it has become an unfair imposition on old and feeble pensioners, who have to travel unnecessarily, if the branches of these exclusive three financial institutions are far from their residences.

Caring Society

These are only some of the areas where the application of greater efficiency and more priority will go a long way to building a more caring Malaysian society. It is hoped that the Federal and State authorities will draw up Priority Plans for Efficient Service to the Public for the next five years, starting from now.

After all, Malaysians do not ask for much. They deserve more efficient services and self-respect from the Government, to which they have given so much of their overwhelming support. However, the patience of the people can wear out in time. We cannot take it for granted that just because they are not vociferous that they will also be compliant.

Despite all our accomplishments in economic development, our world-class buildings and now the Multimedia Super Corridor, it is the people who will judge ultimately whether the government has delivered. We cannot fail them.

16.

LEADERSHIP IDEALS
FOR MALAYSIA

LEADERSHIP ideals in Malaysia are quite unique because Malaysian society is unique. True, there are many countries that have multiracial, multireligious and multicultural societies. But I dare say that it is difficult to find a country that has such a complex combination of races, religions and cultures to the same extent and degree as in Malaysia. Here our minorities are large and significant. According to the latest census figures, Malaysia had a population of 19.4 million people in 1995. Indigenous Bumiputeras (largely ethnic Malays) comprised 62 per cent of the total, Chinese 27 per cent, Indians 8 per cent, and others 3 per cent. Therefore, the rights of the minorities have to be taken seriously.

Thus leadership ideals in Malaysia can be very complicated and difficult to achieve. The following are some of the leadership ideals required in Malaysia.

Leadership Ideals

First, Malaysian leaders have to be fair and reasonable. They must not be leaders of their own race alone, but have to be nationalistic and conscious of the needs, aspirations and sensitivities of all the other races as well.

Second, Malay leaders, in particular, because they wield most of the power, as the majority race, cannot be arrogant or selfish. They have to fight the temptation to submit to the pressures of extremist groups based on race and religion. It would be catastrophic if UMNO is not liberal, as there would be instability and chaos, as we have seen in many other multiracial societies.

Third, leaders have to be honest and open with each other quietly. If they make their divergent views known publicly, then there are those who will exploit these views for personal gain. Thus, the honest expression of racial anxieties should not be expressed openly, but in private and preferably behind closed doors. This is the secret behind the tremendous success of the Barisan Nasional Government, an alliance or coalition of about fifteen political parties. Though sometimes they have strong differences in content, style and approach to problems, they work out compromises on a realistic basis. Decisions are made on the basis of pragmatism. Policies that are only acceptable to all groups are adopted. Decisions are not based on the principle of desirability of the majority, but on the consensus of all.

Fourth, leaders must set high standards of morality and good conduct. We have to set good examples if we want to lead effectively. Of course, politicians are also human and many fail the test of leadership by example. But the ideals remain. The high standards must be used as benchmarks and good leaders should strive hard to follow these ideal standards.

Fifth, leaders of today have to be knowledgeable. They have to speak effectively in at least one of the international languages, preferably in English. They must be able to argue and persuade with facts and figures and in the English idiom, with all its subtleties. Otherwise, their leadership and capacity to influence and lead in international fora will be jeopardised. We would otherwise be just another small developing country that would be taken for granted.

Sixth, our leaders must have vision. We can't lead effectively if we do not have a long-term perspective and a long-range vision. It is this vision that will enable us to set new horizons for our followers and our people. We cannot afford to look just beyond our noses. We cannot be short term in our leadership nor merely expedient in our strategies. We have to be resolute in the pursuit of our long-term vision and goals.

Seventh, according to a Chinese saying, when a fish gets bad, the rot starts at the nervous system in the head. The values and qualities of a person and a nation are largely shaped by the values and qualities of its leadership. It is therefore vital that leaders should pursue the ideals of integrity and sacrifice.

A corrupt leader in whatever field, whether in politics, the professions or in business, will surely erode his or her leadership and that of those whom they lead. Indeed, society itself will crumble over time through corruption. History is full of examples of the rise and fall of nations because of corruption.

Eighth, sacrifice must be the hallmark of a good leader. He has to sacrifice his time, energy and sometimes his own health and welfare for his people—if he is to be a leader of calibre. Many leaders think they can rise to the top without having to make any sacrifices. That is why many leaders fail. Leadership is first and always a special responsibility. The people also expect leaders to sacrifice as a return for their loyalty. It is regarded as an occupational hazard for a leader. People believe that those who cannot sacrifice for the general good of the people should not aspire to be leaders, especially in politics. Leadership has to be earned through sacrifice. There is simply no shortcut.

Ninth, political leadership should be regarded as a privilege to serve the people. People put their trust when electing leaders. Leaders cannot or should not betray that trust. If they do, they deserve to be thrown out of office. However, there are many politicians around the world who perpetuate their power and position by foul means. But these kind of politicians do not last. And even when they do, their reputations become tainted. People lose respect for them and despise them. Such unscrupulous politicians soon grow to despise themselves and fade away in disgrace.

Able Prime Ministers
In Malaysia, we have been fortunate with our political leaders. Our prime ministers, from Tunku Abdul Rahman, Tun Abdul Razak Hussein and Tun Hussein Onn to Dato Seri Dr Mahathir Mohamad,

have all been most appropriate for their time in the evolution of Malaysia's history. Their style of leadership and policies have suited the circumstances of their times in most impressive ways. Consequently, leaders in the civil service and business fit well into the mould of our prime ministers' modes of leadership.

Leadership Ideals and Weaknesses

However, regardless of whether leadership is in the political, professional, civil service or business fields, there are many common values that must be prerequisites for leadership that I have already outlined. The other values and ideals for good leadership are outlined below.

First, there must be focus to succeed. Too often potential leaders fizzle out because they tried to achieve too many objectives at the same time. Often these objectives were inconsistent and conflicting.

Second, leaders must have the determination and stamina to excel. They start off with great ideas but give up too easily when they encounter obstacles. If they try hard to overcome these obstacles, they often give up after losing stamina. They refuse to pick up the pieces and push forward to overcome problems and strive to excel.

Third, when leaders succeed, they sometimes tend to become complacent. They often become over-confident and forget the sense of purpose and direction that brought them success.

Fourth, some business leaders get greedy. Greed destroys them. They over-extend themselves and cannot keep up with their expansion programmes. The span of control of their operations gets out of hand and their effectiveness weakens. They should not overdo.

Finally, the biggest problem leaders have is the lack of effective and loyal lieutenants and support staff. The best leadership can suffer if their aides let them down through disloyalty, inefficiency, indifference and dubious advice. That is why it is essential that leaders have to be constantly vigilant about the standards and quality of their staff. One bad apple can spoil the whole case. Dissatisfaction and disloyalty must be nipped in the bud.

Leaders have to lead. The ideal for leaders is therefore to strive to continue to lead if they choose to continue to be leaders. However, as time passes, challenges change and the capacity necessary to face the challenges also change. Hence, leaders will need to exercise greater sense of discretion and timing; to know when they have reached the peak of their performance in serving the people and the nation.

PART FOUR

SOCIO-ECONOMIC ISSUES

17.

CORRUPTION AND ITS DANGERS

CORRUPTION goes back a long way. Corruption is widespread. It is difficult to find a place on earth where you cannot find corruption of one kind or another. It is only a matter of degree and form.

The western press makes it out as if corruption is typical of or peculiar to the Third World. It might be true that it is more widespread and pernicious in many developing countries. But it can also be found in worse forms in many western countries in the past while they were themselves developing. Indeed, even today, in many advanced countries like Italy and many East European countries, corruption is widespread. In the United States, corruption is widely practised by the lobbyists but there they call corruption commissions or professional fees for services rendered!

That is why Malaysia is rated by some analysts somewhere in the middle of the corruption scale, in between the best examples of minimal corruption and the worst cases of raging corruption.

What is Corruption?
Corruption is described as "a bribe, to make putrid, to taint or to deprave someone", in order to get some benefit. Given this strict definition of corruption, we can ask whether in absolute terms, how many of us are free from corruption. How many times have we even as children been given sweets to keep quiet or not to tell on our elder brothers or sisters.

That is a kind of corruption. We give and receive presents from our neighbours and friends, often because we expect to get something bigger in return. That is corruption of one kind or another which has always been there. It is as old as the hills. It is a fine line between a bribe and a genuine gift!

The dividing line gets thicker between a bribe and a gift when the gift costs much more than a nominal gift or when the recipient is someone of authority and influence, from whom we expect to get a favour or special consideration in return.

Who is involved?

The recipient of a corrupt gift could be a government official who issues licenses. It could be a politician who can influence policy to ensure that some business interests are protected for a friend or partner. It could even happen between one businessmen and another for mutual benefit, but often at the expense of the companies they work for. Contracts for supplies of equipment and services are often rigged, so that both buyers and sellers in different companies benefit, without the knowledge of top management or shareholders. The point I am making is that corruption can be widespread in the private sector. However, the public is not necessarily aware since the people involved rarely complain—because both sides benefit.

But in Government, corrupt officials are more vulnerable to detection and apprehension because the rules and regulations are far more stringent. Furthermore, the checks and balances in the government machinery are extensive, but often stifle action and initiative. This weakness is also the strength in Government administration, as corruption can be better controlled with stringent controls and supervision. However, corruption is extremely difficult to eliminate.

Today, corruption has become even more subtle. It can take place at the golf course where officials on both sides and within the public and private sectors can bet heavily and deliberately lose, to pass money on to the other party with great subtlety.

Some people even buy lottery tickets at a premium from genuine winners in order to keep "evidence" of so-called winnings which are actually slush funds. I have heard people joking that someone is "always lucky as he wins the lotteries so often".

Corruption is not only confined to government officials, politicians and businessmen. Professionals also indulge in it. Doctors are known to liberally give medical certificates and false medical reports to facilitate insurance claims for special considerations. Engineers and consultants sometimes cut corners or divulge vital information to contractors bidding for a tender. Some lawyers have been found to fiddle with clients' funds and indulge in corrupt practices. There are even allegations of some judges being involved. So corruption is found anywhere in society. This is true not only in Malaysia but in all countries, to a greater or lesser degree. There is hardly any country that is free from the tentacles of corruption.

Why does corruption occur?
Corruption of the scale it is today is relatively new to Malaysia. In the past when incomes were much lower and income disparity was narrower, corruption was far less significant. Previously, the economy was slow moving, business was conducted at a low level and the opportunities for corruption were therefore much less. Today, with rapid economic growth, widening income disparity, inflation and big billion-dollar contracts, the lure of corruption has become vastly more significant.

Values have also changed. Corruption used to be frowned upon, if not scowled at. However, now the sensitivity to corruption is much less. Many think it is the in-thing and that those in sensitive areas are silly not to take advantage of the opportunities for corruption. Others regard it as a convenient form of transferring incomes from the richer to the poorer sectors of society. Some wrongly regard corruption as a smart practice.

Corruption is also a function of rising materialism. Here again values have changed. People with wealth and not intellect, piety or wisdom, are given more time and respect. Often an uneducated rogue with a big house and a shiny car is accorded more respect than an honest, decent professional. So the tendency is to go for more money, whatever the means to that end. To the money-minded and those obsessed with greed and becoming wealthy fast, corruption is the answer. And many go for it in a big way. This is sad for corruption weakens the nation.

What are the consequences of corruption?

There is no doubt that corruption is cancerous. It eats into the very cells of society and ultimately, if not suppressed, grows and destroys the very foundation of society.

Corruption undermines the quest for excellence. Why excel, some argue, when one can gain material wealth easily through corrupt practices. This negative attitude breeds a culture of poor quality and incompetence. It also erodes meritocracy and creates a culture of mediocrity.

Corruption causes social inequalities and leads to social unrest. Corrupt individuals get rich quickly without much effort. Someone who is relatively poor can become rich overnight through corruption. He is therefore catapulted to the ranks of the rich, many of whom may have struggled long and hard to get to the top. Corruption can widen the gap between the rich and the poor even faster. If this happens the whole purpose of the New Economic Policy and the National Development Policy which aim to reduce income inequality regardless of race will be defeated. The NDP itself could be undermined.

Corruption can cause ethnic tensions due to ethnic-based income inequality. This could lead to political instability due to consequent racial tension and antagonism. Corruption can also erode the economy. It breeds inefficiencies in the system and adversely affects productivity. More will be spent unnecessarily to get relatively less output. This is because more of the funds will be diverted to unproductive purposes, just as incomes will be transferred to individuals who will be unproductive agents who do not produce the goods and services that are income-generating. If more and more finds are spent to merely grease the system, then the nation's production targets will not be met. Economic growth will then be stifled and the 7.5 per cent annual growth rates envisaged by Vision 2020 could be undermined.

Inflation will be even more difficult to contain or restrain with growing corruption. As more funds are corruptly paid out from production to the consumption points, all along the distribution system, the costs will rise. This could cause unnecessary cost-push effects and raise prices. Fiscal and monetary measures cannot be effective in a regime of excessive corruption. Only anti-corruption measures can combat price increases that are due to corruption. But once corruption gets hold of a society, even anti-corruption measures cannot help much. Prevention is therefore much more effective than the cure for corruption.

Malaysia's concept of a Caring Society can be seriously eroded by corruption. How can the people feel cared for if the poor see those in authority get richer at their expense. How can the corrupt, who are basically greedy and selfish, be expected to care for the less fortunate.

Given that the nation's Gross Domestic Product is about RM140 billion and that corruption occurs both in the public as well as the private sectors, if 5 per cent of the GDP is spent on corruption, then about RM7 billion can be hypothetically estimated as the amount wasted on corruption every year. Is this estimate too low or too high? If it is a reasonable assumption, then think of the vast amounts of money that could have otherwise been spent on social causes, like more schools, hospitals and housing for the poorest of our society.

What can be done then to reduce corruption?
It may be difficult, if not impossible, to reduce corruption to zero. No country in the world has succeeded in wiping out corruption, prostitution or drugs, even when the penalty is death. Corruption can however be reduced, if not eliminated. This can be achieved through improved values and a corruption-free culture through education. This educational process must start at home, during the early stages of building values, right through the school and religious systems of education, up to the tertiary levels of learning.

All religions teach honesty and rejection of corruption. Thus, much more can be done through the religions of all communities to build a stronger sense of rejection and repugnance to corruption. Religious teaching at schools and moral instruction should stress the evils of corruption and promote contempt for and the rejection of corruption. However, it is important that our leaders set high standards in fighting corruption through their words and deeds. It is not helpful to teach our children of the evils of corruption and then expose them to adults and particularly leaders who may be involved in corruption. Our slogan "Leadership by Example" should be observed and adhered to strictly, with regard to fighting corruption.

Excessive regulation provides fertile grounds for corruption. For every rule and regulation, the corrupt will find many ways and means to go round the regulations through corrupt means. Too many rules stifle business activity, initiative and profits. Thus, businessmen will make it their business to corrupt those in power and subvert the regulations. The more liberal the economy, the fewer the rules that are necessary. Then there will be fewer opportunities for corruption. We must therefore liberalise the economy more and become more competitive.

Malaysia should therefore reduce the vast array of rules and regulations and the obstacles to competition. This is not to say that we must become *laissez faire* or completely free of rules and regulations. The free market system has, by its very nature, built-in weaknesses and market imperfections. What we need to do is to review and revise our rules and regulations that inhibit trade and investment. We need to eliminate or reduce outdated and unnecessary obstacles to business. The gradual reduction of import duties will contribute greatly to the reduction of corruption in the Royal Customs and Excise and Immigration Departments. Similarly, other areas of business would benefit from more transparency and less regulations.

This is another reason why the National Development Policy must be modified and made more transparent. Preferential treatment breeds pseudo-partnerships that are created through a kind of corruption. The allocation of free or highly undervalued pink shares to vested groups is not productive. This can be considered as some variation of corruption. Instead of giving these so-called pink certificates to individuals, they could be given to large groups of investors through the Amanah Saham

Nasional, the Amanah Saham Wawasan 2020 and other investment funds. This would be more equitable and transparent. More importantly, it will reduce corruption.

Finally, corruption has to be significantly reduced if not eliminated, if Malaysia is to continue to progress and succeeded. Corruption is found both in the public and private sectors. The degree of corruption is still not too serious in Malaysia. However, the trends are discouraging. If these adverse trends worsen, then we will not be able to achieve the aspirations of Vision 2020. It is the duty of all Malaysians to fight corruption for our own well-being, as well as the survival and progress of the nation. Given the will, we can reduce corruption significantly.

The battle against corruption has begun in earnest, with the Prime Minister Dato Seri Dr Mahathir Mohamad taking the lead in fighting money politics in UMNO. Indeed, other political parties should also follow UMNO's good example.

If the political leaders and the political parties clean up corruption successfully within the political system then there is great hope that Malaysia will succeed in the campaign against corruption.

18.

ENVIRONMENTAL DECLINE

IN recent years, we have increasingly questioned the quality of our economic development. Is it adversely affecting our environment? Is our economic success only for the short term? Can our development be sustained?

Sustainable development is a relatively new concept to us and even worldwide. Only after the Rio Earth Summit in 1992 did people all over the world become more seriously aware of the hazards of environmental pollution and its threat to mankind's well-being—and survival.

I believe that the Malaysian Government is committed to sustainable development. But how serious or successful have we been?

What is sustainable development? It is best described by the Brudtland Commission as "Development that meets the needs of the present without compromising the ability of future generations to meet their needs."

Based on this definition, I believe that we are moving towards sustainable development but at an unacceptably slow pace. Unless we strengthen our policies and environmental laws, and enforce them effectively, Malaysia's economic development could gradually lose its sustainability. If our natural resources like land, bio-diversity, water resources, timber, petroleum and gas are depleted and destroyed, the needs of future generations will not be met. The aspirations of Vision 2020 will not be achieved on target, if we neglect our environment.

But why are we not able to do more to protect our God-given environment, which we all cherish, but which many of us tend to neglect and destroy. Why?

First, there is a general misconception that our environment is still comparatively clean. We think that as a developing country, since manufacturing constitutes only about 30 per cent of the economy, pollution from manufacturing cannot do too much damage as yet. So there is plenty of time before we start worrying about serious pollution and environmental damage.

Second, the Department of Environment (DOE) has not been given adequate attention or priority. Its resources could definitely be strengthened. Its Annual Reports state that its work has increased but its staff reduced! So how can the DOE effectively enforce the country's environmental rules and regulations? This is why there have been so many abuses of the environment that have been committed with impunity. Even the Prime Minister has publicly stated that his advice on the clearing of hill slopes have been repeatedly ignored. We see plenty of evidence all over; see what happened at Genting Highlands and the North-South Highway near Tapah, Perak. Even the hills at the Universiti of Malaya have been cleared and made bald!

Third, businessmen generally do not have a value system and culture of environmental protection. Instead, many of them see environmental exploitation as a means to get rich quickly. They are generally only interested in fulfilling their own short-term needs. But there are exceptions, of course.

Fourth, Malaysians are not adequately educated on environmental matters. The poor may be excused because they are primarily concerned with survival. They cannot be expected to think of the environment at the risk of losing their livelihood. But what about the educated, the well-to-do and particularly, the rich? They have no excuse and deserve to be condemned for neglecting and exploiting the environment.

Fifth, the Government itself can and should do more. Indeed, the concern for the environment was led by the Government. But it seems to be stymied by vested interests—greedy and influential business groups, some of whom finance some election candidates especially at the lower levels of Government.

Prime Minister Dato Seri Dr Mahathir Mohamad showed great initiative in launching the Langkawi Declaration on Environment. But he cannot do much all by himself. The DOE, under Minister Law Hieng Ding, and former Director-General Dato' Dr Abu Bakar Jaafar, has achieved a great deal in its short history. But they too cannot do it alone.

Deterioration

Then who can give greater push to protect the environment? I believe it is the people—the man in the street. Only the people in a democracy like ours can demand and get what they want from our society. It is People's Power that counts in the final analysis. But our people as a whole have been quite complacent.

Let us review our environmental record. This is important as it has a direct bearing on the sustainability of our economic development. Furthermore, if we do not adequately prevent environmental degradation now, the costs of environmental correction later could become very costly and even prohibitive.

According to DOE Reports, water pollution has worsened. Our rivers and coastal waters suffer serious pollution. Earthworks have been the major cause of pollution. Developers and contractors, including our professional architects and engineers, constitute the biggest culprits. This is sad because these professionals should be the most committed to protecting the environment, instead of exploiting it.

Air quality is poor. Vehicular emission of lorries, buses and taxis using diesel are the major sources of pollution (36 per cent). Open burning is another major source of pollution. But why can't this pollution be reduced? Is it poor enforcement, vested interests, corruption, outdated engines or mere ignorance? The DOE would need to study the causes of this poor air quality to be able to deal with these problems effectively. But merely going for more and more reports without proper enforcement is of no real use.

Noise pollution is worsening. The noise levels in most of our populated areas exceed the World Health Organisation's recommended levels. This is a real shame for a country that is an example of socio-economic progress in the Third World! Our noise level is in the range of 43.6aB(A)-81.1aB(A), which is very high and unhealthy.

River water pollution is rising. The Water Quality Index indicates that our river water quality has been deteriorating at 1.9 per cent per annum. How can we be proud of this record? What is the use of economic development, if our environment gets destroyed? No wonder the price of fish keeps rising, as our fish are killed in our rivers and surrounding seas by pollution.

Indeed, our rising cost of living could be partially attributed to water, land and air pollution. This is a great loss to the economy and its potential and sustainability. And the poor suffer the most.

Marine environmental quality: oil and grease (E. coli) and total suspended solids (TSS) are high in our coastal waters. TSS has increased to 34 per cent per site per year. E. coli has also deteriorated at 10 per cent per site per annum. Thus our marine environmental quality is deteriorating quite badly. Should we not give higher priority to combat this deterioration? What is holding us back?

Proposed Measures

A great deal has been done to combat pollution and to help sustain our economic development. However, much more needs to be done.

First, we need stronger people's participation. The Government, NGOs, the DOE and the Department of Irrigation and Drainage need to be backed up by more concerned and active public campaigns against pollution.

Second, the major indicators of pollution would need to be highlighted and benchmarked on a more frequent basis, such as Quarterly Reports by the DOE. The Press could have weekly columns on Pollution Watch to alert the public and highlight cases of blatant abuse of the environment. They should follow up until the authorities do something about overcoming environmental threats.

Third, commercial banks should get into the act and refrain from financing projects that pollute. If they do not fulfil their corporate responsibilities, then the Government could instruct them to withdraw from financing projects that cause pollution. But why can't banks exercise self-regulation for the public interest. After all, banks do make a great deal of profits from the public. Banks could ask for Environmental Reports.

Fourth, penalties for pollution must be raised further to effectively curtail pollution. The existing small fines provide little disincentives. The courts should exercise a greater sense of perspective and impose tougher deterrents on polluters. The present fines even against the dumping of cyanide are most discouraging and demoralising.

Fifth, the Treasury has to be more stringent in allocating funds for development that is not sustainable. The Treasury should be tougher in its criteria for allocations. Funds should not be allocated for environmentally questionable projects.

Sixth, the enforcement authorities, especially the Department of Environment and the Department of Irrigation and Drainage, have to be strengthened and given more Government support. Otherwise it becomes a mockery, if they do not perform effectively due to a lack of staff and equipment.

Seventh, the quality of life should be given higher priority in the planning and implementation of Government Budgets and Five-Year Plans, to sustain socio-economic development. Otherwise government policies will lose their credibility.

Eighth, the State Governments will have to be forced by the Federal Government to give much higher priority to combating environmental damage, especially in land utilisation and management. If they do not, then penalise them through the reduction of development funds and grants.

Every parliamentary and state constituency should have an Environmental Watch Group, which could pressure their elected representatives and those on local councils to protect and preserve our beautiful environment for posterity.

Otherwise, our impressive growth and development will not be sustained. We must act now before it is too late. We have to show a higher commitment to protect our environment for posterity. The Government has to take a stronger lead to protect our enviable environment. The Government must be more serious in introducing and implementing better policies to combat pollution more effectively. The people on their part must push the Government through Peoples' Power to do a better job in fighting pollution.

19.
LISTENING TO THE PEOPLE

USUALLY, any new Government spells out its new plan of action or its new deal within the first 100 days after the General Elections. Now the people ask, what will the government do for them in return for the powerful mandate they have given to the Barisan Nasional Government at the General Elections.

Are we going to get more of the same? If that is the case, then why was so much power given to the Government? The people expect more. There must not only be more of the same. Expectations have risen and justifiably so. Many also ask whether the Government would be as attentive to public concerns. Will it be sensitive and as caring as before? It is said that power corrupts. We are nowhere near absolute power, but the power the Government has, is nevertheless overwhelming. Few Governments ever obtain a majority of two-thirds in Parliament.

Checks and Balances
Checks and balances will be less than before, now that the people have stifled the Opposition. The Opposition could sit back and say, "Let them do their worst. We'll watch and wait."

If the Government's performance and service to the *rakyat* fall short, the electoral pendulum could then move the other way.

This swing has occurred before, not here, but elsewhere. Its possibility will be greater if the current favourable economic outlook turns sour.

This is not improbable as the world's largest economies—the United States and Japan—can falter and fight each other on the economic front.

Trade and currency conflicts are constantly raging between these two mighty economies, and this is a cause for concern. Despite Malaysia's outstanding economic performance, its economy is relatively small and is subject to the vagaries of the global economic climate. We have to be alert and agile. We, like the proverbial *pelanduk* (mousedeer), could be caught in-between, when the two elephants fight it out (*"Gajah sama gajah berjuang, pelanduk mati ditengah-tengah"*).

There is a growing feeling that some Federal and State authorities are not listening adequately to public concerns and complaints. What are the other channels of communication to the powers that be, if elected members do not act upon our concerns? The opposition representatives are unlikely to be heard by the authorities. So what recourse is there for the *rakyat*, if elected representatives do not respond to their aspirations?

The mass media is the only recourse if they are encouraged to play their role. It is in the interests of the Government to have an open and responsible media. It could therefore do more to encourage greater independence of the media to obtain better feedback.

Prime Minister Dato Seri Dr Mahathir Mohamad has introduced a Code of Ethics for Ministers. Thus, the people and media should fulfil their obligations by monitoring the performance of our leaders. Indeed the State Governments and civil servants should be monitored for the quality of their service against this Code and the civil servants' charter of performance.

Ombudsman

We might want to reconsider the appointment of an Ombudsman, who could be directly responsible to the Prime Minister. This way the Code of Ethics can be administered effectively at all levels of Government.

I have mentioned some major basic inefficiencies that need to be addressed. There are a few more.

First, women's rights. They are better here than in other countries but why is it that half our population does not have equitable and fair legislation? Some of the laws that discriminate against women include those relating to rape, domestic violence, custody, guardianship and maintenance of children, inheritance and property rights, and immigration laws, concerning the employment of foreign wives. But I wonder why our womenfolk are not forceful enough on what is surely their birth right—to be treated fairly. Most men would support their cause if they could get the men to be more involved.

Second, it is disappointing that our voting registration numbers were recorded on the counterfoils of our ballot papers on the last Election Day. The Chairman of the Elections Commission Dato' Harun Din said the practice is legal and it is necessary in order to follow up on any subsequent protests. But surely the whole principle of the secrecy of the vote is violated. There must be other ways to deal with this problem without having to cast doubts on the voting process, and more importantly, the secrecy of the ballot.

Third, our privatised and corporatised entities could be more efficient. The argument has been that it is difficult for Government departments to be very efficient because of the plethora of rules and regulations. But are the privatised utilities more efficient now? They have become more conscious of making more money. Fees and charges have gone up, but has efficiency gone up? I doubt it.

Tenaga Nasional Berhad recently wanted to raise its rates. I agree with the Federation of Malaysian Consumer Associations (FOMCA) president Hamdan Adnan that there was no justification for higher rates, especially when efficiency is wanting. The Government was wise to scrap the tariff increases. What Tenaga National and other public utilities should do is to control costs rather than increase rates. If the privatised entities were open to more competition, they would be more efficient, and also more profitable. The recent electricity blackout peninsula-wide tells a lot about Tenaga Nasional's efficiency. Hopefully, the investigation into the causes of the breakdown will throw some light on this issue and not leave us in the dark.

What happened with the electricity breakdown is, to say the least, very sad. There should have been much more priority given to maintenance. In fact, the Government should seriously consider setting up an overall authority to monitor and supervise all privatisation projects to ensure cost savings and efficient services. The Government could regulate its own privatised utilities to set better standards of efficiency and corporate responsibility. Then the other large corporations can be urged to follow suit. Better still, some of the large privatised utilities and corporations could be broken down into smaller units to provide competition within them. We all know monopolies breed inefficiencies. Thus, privatised entities could turn out to be worse than when the Government ran these companies.

Fourth, environmental regulations are not being efficiently enforced. Our air, rivers, land and seas are getting more polluted. All this can be prevented by heavier penalties and better enforcement. It is good that air and water pollution monitoring centres are being privatised. But merely monitoring environmental degradation will not be meaningful if we do not at the same time have the will to combat pollution. We need the same zeal that has been summoned to fight inflation. Lax enforcement will lead to serious damage not only to the environment and national self-respect but to the economy in the longer term.

Fifth, flooding, especially in squatter areas, is a recurring problem. Why should poor families be subjected to so much misery and neglect? Why should they be forced to become poorer each time flooding occurs? If we can provide funds for mega projects, why can't we divert smaller amounts for flood alleviation?

New Initiatives

The Deputy Prime Minister Dato' Seri Anwar Ibrahim recently announced a new package to liberalise the capital market. This is most welcome as it signals even more competition for the economy. More competition will reduce inefficiency and provide better services.

New policy initiatives have also been taken by new Minister of Education Dato' Seri Mohd Najib Tun Abdul Razak Hussein in emphasising the importance of English and technical education. I wish more ministries would unfold new and better policy initiatives as soon as possible to benefit the people.

It will be gratifying if all Members of Parliament can have their own Constituency Action Programmes that can be implemented before the next general elections. The people need to be heard and served better.

We could re-establish the old *Red Book* technique that was so successfully used by the late Prime Minister, Tun Abdul Razak Hussein. This way, these action programmes and the new code of ethics could also be effectively monitored and implemented even more meaningfully.

We would need an Operations Room in every constituency to set out new policy and implementation targets that could be closely observed by the electorate and the Prime Minister's Department. This is only fair and just.

Domestic Violence Act 1995

The Domestic Violence Act 1995 will finally be implemented. This is most welcome. With this move, women's rights in Malaysia took a big leap forward because there's now recourse for women who have to endure domestic abuse, both physically and mentally. Socio-economic progress and well-being will not be possible without the support of our womenfolk. Successful economic management and modernisation have been achieved largely because of the contribution of women. Their capability for strengthening the family and nation-building must therefore be preserved and protected.

Our women have every right to expect fair and equal treatment. How can they effectively contribute to nation-building if they feel a sense of deprivation. I have encountered many women in the course of my working life who feel discriminated against and so become demotivated in their careers.

The problems faced by our women are not theirs alone. They are overall national socio-economic and human problems. I wonder what our reaction would be if the problems, which led to the Domestic Violence Act being enacted, were experienced by the men. Are we slow in our response or weak in our will to provide justice to women, since men are not directly involved? Are we less responsive because most political leaders and legislators are men, and therefore, they may not empathise with the aspirations of women and the problems they face?

I would think that our women should assert themselves more strongly and purposefully for their legitimate rights. They could seek the help and support of VIP women, the wives of VIPs and women leaders in government and business, to expedite the implementation of the regulations relating to the fair and equal treatment of all women. But the relevant authorities will need to be more tolerant and positively disposed to constructive criticism. Otherwise, frustration will grow and discontentment will spread.

The Government will therefore need to give much greater priority to these serious and sensitive issues relating to women. All pending legislation must be closely monitored and finalised soon to give our women a better deal. This is necessary in order to enhance the confidence of our womenfolk in the capacity of our system to provide justice and promote the welfare of all Malaysian women.

Then we can reasonably expect our women to take on wider and heavier responsibilities in the modernisation and economic development of our country to better achieve the aspirations of Vision 2020. This will also be our opportunity and our challenge as we move towards being a more Caring Society.

20.
SOCIAL DEVELOPMENT AND POVERTY

MALAYSIA IS one of the very few Third World countries that was able to make a major contribution at the World Summit on Social Development in Copenhagen, Denmark, in 1995. Our Prime Minister Dato Seri Dr Mahathir Mohamad no doubt made a positive impact there. But Malaysia too can learn more and improve further. We can do even more to change for the better, though our poverty eradication record has been quite impressive.

We have indeed come a long way since just after *Merdeka* when we used to ask for help from multinational aid consortia for our socio-economic development. Unfortunately, many other countries still have to depend on aid and therefore cannot and do not speak up for fear of aid cutbacks.

Today, we do not need nor want aid but fair trade. We have pulled ourselves by our own bootstraps to become one of the best examples of successful economic and social development.

Thus we have not had to subject ourselves to tight structural adjustment programmes of the World Bank or the International Monetary Fund (IMF). Under these programmes, countries often have to raise taxes sharply, drastically cut down expenditures and domestic and especially foreign borrowing. All these measures are imposed to reduce budget and balance of payments deficits in order to qualify for soft or low interest rate loans from the World Bank or the IMF. These radical measures have often caused even more social misery to the poor countries in the short term. This is why many have criticised the World Bank and the IMF for their insensitivity.

Sometimes these developing countries have drifted into real trouble due to their own political and economic mismanagement, especially in countries where natural resources are poor. Where they have rich resources, many have squandered them.

But many countries also get into serious economic difficulties because the rich industrial countries block their imports with high protectionist tariff and non-tariff walls. Even now they try to introduce so-called 'social clauses' to make it easier for them and more difficult for the Third World.

Malaysia is indeed much better off. We are less dependent on the vagaries of the prices of our primary commodities as 80 per cent of our exports are now in manufactured goods. We can thus appreciate the problems faced by those developing countries that are going through the painful process of socio-economic growth and development that we have been through before.

The main thrust of the Social Development Conference was to seek ways to reduce poverty and unemployment to promote social integration. On both the first two counts we have done very well, although there is much more to be achieved. But on social integration we have a longer way to go.

Poverty
With regard to poverty, Malaysia's achievements in reducing poverty from 1.1 million in 1970 to 0.6 million in 1990 is impressive. But there is still much scope for improvement. Living just above the poverty line is no comfort either. There are thousands of our citizens in *kampungs*, new villages, estates and the depressed urban areas, who are marginalised. These relatively poor groups are just above subsistence income levels, with low literacy and low skills. They are not very mobile in the labour market. They will be the least able to move upward socially and economically.

150

The key to socio-economic mobility is better education. If the rural and urban poor children go to the government and private school systems, at least until the Penilaian Menengah Rendah (PMR) level (up to about 15 years of age), then there is hope for them. But unfortunately, there is a high dropout rate especially among those who attend badly staffed private schools, like Tamil schools in the estates, where their future is bleak.

In these cases the children are doomed to lives of low income, low esteem and menial work. They will be the weakest links in the socio-economic chain of progress, especially as Malaysia becomes more industrialised.

In fact these underprivileged and marginalised citizens could well become Malaysia's underclass. They would not be able to find employment in the productive and competitive sectors of the economy, and could well cause a drag on the nation's socio-economic development.

It is thus vital to provide more educational and training facilities to these potential dropouts. A better educated labour force would prevent dependence on foreign labour and help to promote socio-economic growth on a sustained basis.

Unemployment

Malaysia already has almost full employment. The estimated 2.8 per cent unemployment is really structural, in that it covers those who are not willing or not able to work. There could be some seasonal unemployment included. Thus, there are hardly any problems of unemployment, unlike most industrialised countries, which are plagued with serious structural unemployment.

But there can be considerable weaknesses in the Malaysian labour force. For instance, is our labour force productive enough? Does it employ sufficient technology? Is it internationally competitive? Could its educational levels be raised to absorb higher skills? Are training and research and development facilities sufficient to encourage labour to be more efficient?

These are some of the critical issues that must be addressed. Otherwise Malaysia will continue to produce labour intensive products and slowly but surely lose its competitiveness to Thailand and Indonesia.

We cannot therefore be satisfied with just near full employment. We have to push for better quality employment with higher productivity.

Social Disintegration
The third objective of the Social Development Conference was to achieve social integration and prevent social disintegration. This is a growing problem in Malaysia.

Social disintegration, although not serious now, can become critical, as it has become acute in many industrialised countries. The breakdown of traditional values and family ties is becoming more apparent.

Waywardness, drugs, juvenile crime, child and spouse abuse are all on the rise. Evidence of social indifference is seen in road bullying, inconsiderate driving and the careless disposal of garbage in our rivers, streets and drains. Social discipline has been sliding.

National Unity
It is also questionable whether national unity has been increasing or declining over the years. Are we more or less compartmentalised or polarised than before? Are we approaching the point where our national unity and competitiveness are being eroded by our well meant socio-economic policies?

This is why it is important to adopt a Socio-Economic Index that will tell us where we are in the ladder of social development and national unity and how much progress we are making towards greater social integration. Unless we monitor and measure our social progress, we will be having noble objectives and pious hopes but nothing much could be happening or achieved.

We do not have to measure our progress in social development through the discredited UNDP Social Index, but we should devise our own Social Index and work hard towards raising our social standards and Malaysia's quality of life.

Thus, we should really aim to build a Malaysian Model of Social Development that we can be proud of, and which other countries may want to emulate. With the right political will, we can.

But what can Malaysia learn from the Social Development Conference? What follow-up action can we take?

For one thing, we could do more to offer our services to those developing countries that could benefit from our successful socio-economic experiences. But more importantly, we could do more by ourselves for our own people. So what should we do here in Malaysia?

First, our fiscal and monetary policies could be revised to make them even more people oriented. The Government's Budget revenues and expenditures could be refined to give even more priority to socio-economic development, especially since we have built up high Budget surpluses. More allocations could be made for basic needs such as education, health, housing, agriculture, drainage and irrigation and better amenities can be provided for the poorer citizens in both the rural and urban areas.

We should increasingly emphasise a more 'basic needs' approach that could directly benefit the poorer people. This could be aimed to eliminate poverty within a time frame of say 10 years by 2005. We can surely do it, given our resources, strong leadership and our rich religious and sound Asian social values.

Second, the private sector could be encouraged to raise more funds to finance those infrastructure projects that are utilised more by the wealthier sections of the population. More of these projects like schools and hospitals could be privatised and their services could be priced according to the market. After all, those who use high cost facilities like airports and highways should be able to pay for these services that the low income citizens do not often use. The Government could then provide more resources to the people who need help most.

Third, the Government could introduce higher taxes on higher income consumption goods and services. If the more wealthy prefer bigger cars, better housing and other luxury consumption goods and services, let them pay for it through higher taxes such as the Sales tax, and a Value-

Added Tax. These taxes could be exempted for the goods and services consumed by the lower income groups. This would be fair and equitable. We could therefore have a two-tier approach to socio-economic development.

We thus need a paradigm shift in our socio-economic policies in order to increase the social development standards and quality of life of especially our lower income citizens. We must change policies for the greater benefit of our people. After all we now have big Budget surpluses. Let us use more of these surplus funds to promote greater social integration of our people for greater national unity.

21.

NATIONAL UNITY:
A MALAYSIAN INDIAN VIEW

THE Malaysian nation was born in 1957, but almost 40 years later, full National Unity is still an unfulfilled major aspiration. The Malaysian Constitution and the Rukunegara laid the foundations to achieve National Unity but the racial riots of May 1969 ruptured any hopes that we had achieved it, at that time. We still do not have a Bangsa Malaysia or a Malaysian Race.

The New Economic Policy in 1970 aimed to set new directions to help achieve National Unity. However, about 25 years later, many Malaysian Indians think that the NEP has brought about greater Malay or Bumiputera benefits and solidarity, but ironically a greater sense of alienation amongst the other races.

Then in 1991, the National Development Policy (NDP) and Dato Seri Dr Mahathir Mohamad's Vision 2020 were designed to improve upon the NEP, to achieve the same objective of building National Unity more purposefully, through the process of developing Malaysia into an industrialised nation by the year 2020. The predominant priority and underlying thrust of Vision 2020 is to create a Malaysian Race (*Bangsa Malaysia*). Can this be achieved within the next 25 years?

National Unity today is much more formally pursued than it was at *Merdeka*. Then it was more informal, relaxed, down-to-earth and even more genuine. The Royalty, our National Language, and our active and relatively liberal Democratic System of Government, have all been strong unifying factors. The National Education Policy has, to some extent, strengthened common values and attitudes and helped to evolve some elements of an overall Malaysian Culture and National Unity. However, it will take much longer for these National Unity features to seep through Malaysian Society and to be absorbed by the Soul of its people.

In the meantime, despite the Government's many initiatives to promote National Unity, there have also been strong counter currents of polarisation.

Today, the Bumiputera and non-Bumiputera policies have unfortunately and even inadvertently created greater sensitivities and more consciousness of our differences, rather than our shared ethos, values, identity, and our common destiny. Although the NEP has brought about political stability, it may have also been ethnically divisive, and created the concept and practice of Malay dominance.

Problems and Issues Confronting National Unity

As a result of all these changes since independence, Malaysian Indians, in general, have become even more conscious of a sense of alienation due to various reasons. This is because of their perceptions that they, in general:

1. Constitute the smallest of the large minorities, i.e. about 8 per cent of the population.
2. Have not gained as much as the Malays and Chinese from Malaysia's rapid economic growth, in many areas.
3. Are losing out relatively to the other races, in terms of Government aid for poverty alleviation, income, social status, equity ownership, education and future advancement opportunities.
4. Feel relatively neglected by the Government, especially when compared to the Government's assistance to the Bumiputeras. The Malaysian Chinese have gained indirectly from rapid economic development and Government contracts, through

the use of their longer experience and enterprise in business as well as their connections.

5. Consider their sense of deprivation as more serious since the Malaysian Indian leadership has been too preoccupied with its own internal problems for a long time. Consequently, the Malaysian Indian leadership has not been able to do much to improve the unfortunate plight of the Malaysian Indian estate workers, in particular, and Malaysian Indians, in general.

6. Accept the objectives of Vision 2020 and appreciate the vigorous efforts being undertaken by the Government to modernise and industrialise the country. But it is feared that Malaysian Indians will be forgotten in the modernisation process and would drift down the national socio-economic ladder.

7. Feel a sense of hopelessness and despair in the rubber and oil palm estates and have no alternative if they move out, but to engage themselves in low-productivity jobs in the urban areas.

8. Expect their depressed lives and low standards of living in the estates to continue indefinitely from generation to generation, in a resigned and fatalistic way, unless they migrate to the towns, for which they are ill equipped.

Malaysian Indians and Malaysian National Unity

Under these circumstances of relative neglect, a perceived indifference to their poor plight and a lack of hope and direction, it is difficult to inspire a spirit of Malaysian Unity and pride amongst the poorer Indians, especially those working in estates. This will be true of any race or people, anywhere in the world, under similar circumstances.

The majority of Malaysian Indians in the estates, therefore, just "exist" and live from day to day without any hope or expectation of progress and prosperity, unlike the other Malaysians, who enjoy a greater sense of confidence for the future. They therefore cannot contribute much to National Unity for they feel isolated, excluded and even alienated from the mainstream of Malaysia's overall socio-economic progress.

Enhancing National Unity Amongst Malaysian Indians

Malaysian Indians who have benefited from a good education in Malaysia and abroad have integrated reasonably well into the rich fabric of Malaysian society. They in fact do contribute effectively to the building of National Unity for they are the professionals and the better educated, especially in the urban areas.

Nevertheless, educated Malaysian Indians at and above the Malaysian Certificate of Education (SPM) level or even the Lower Certificate of Education (SRP) may feel they experience the "Third Preference Syndrome". Many feel that they are given job opportunities only after priority has been given to the Bumiputeras and Malaysian Chinese, particularly in the private sector.

But, once Malaysian Indians find employment that is commensurate with their educational levels and training, they are generally satisfied that they have had a reasonably "fair deal". They have consequently felt less and less the sharp sensitivity of any earlier deprivation or discrimination that they might have experienced previously.

It is also necessary to add that many Malaysian Indians generally feel a sense of alienation or discrimination in their employment, both in the Government, and especially in the private sector.

The Malays have the opportunity to work under Malay management, especially in the Government and in Malay or Bumiputera environments. The Malaysian Chinese, particularly in the private sector, generally work under Malaysian Chinese management and amongst predominantly Malaysian Chinese staff. But it is a rare phenomenon for Malaysian Indians to work under Malaysian Indian management, and rarer still, to work amongst mainly Malaysian Indian staff in larger business enterprises. This is because, except for MAIKA (the business enterprise initiated by the Malaysian Indian Congress), there are unfortunately very few large Malaysian Indian corporations in the country.

Malaysian Indians therefore feel some sense of discrimination and even some persecution in many areas of employment. But this feeling is not necessarily confined to places of employment, but more importantly and unfortunately, it is also experienced in the school system. This sense of alienation is felt even more acutely, especially when most Malaysian Indian children are often the least academically qualified, and come from the most depressed socio-economic backgrounds, that is, the rubber and oil palm estates.

Under these circumstances then, can Malaysian Indians, especially those working in the estates, have a high sense of national consciousness and commitment, and can they contribute effectively to National Unity?

Malaysia cannot afford to allow its 1.7 million (about 8 per cent of the population) Malaysian Indians to feel alienated. But the reality is that the majority of them do. Malaysian Unity and *Bangsa Malaysia* can only be as strong as its weakest link. And the Malaysian Indian community is one of Malaysia's weakest links in the economy.

As long as there is no specific blueprint on the part of the Government to alleviate the weak position of the Malaysian Indians, this community will weigh down Malaysia's efforts at achieving the objectives of Vision 2020. The Indians then will be left to pull themselves up by their bootstraps.

The New Economic Policy stressed the need to remove the identification of race with occupation and to alleviate poverty regardless of race. However, there have been limited and inadequate efforts to apply these laudable objectives to the Malaysian Indian community. In fact, the estates have not really been considered as part of the Government's Rural Development Programmes. They continue to be neglected and isolated, and left to the whims and fancies of private estate owners who, in the main, have used Malaysian Indians as "cheap labour" on estates.

Stability and unity in Malaysia will be hampered if the estate labour is neglected and left to decline and decay. The opportunity cost to the nation could be tremendous and wasteful if the Malaysian Indians in the estates are left relatively unproductive, especially as the Malaysian economy continues to prosper and enjoy almost full employment. To the extent that Malaysian Indian labour is not fully utilised, the economy's growth targets of 7 per cent per annum that is planned for Vision 2020 can be seriously jeopardised. The dedicated efforts made to attain National Unity and to achieve *Bangsa Malaysia* could also be seriously impaired.

The Malaysian Indians can and will be able to contribute effectively to enhance National Unity only by bringing them into the mainstream of Malaysia's modernisation. They can contribute towards meeting the nine challenges of Vision 2020, if they are given the opportunities to participate actively.

Profile of the Malaysian Indian Population

Here I will look at the profile of the Malaysian Indian population and look at measures needed to improve their welfare. Malaysian Indians are primarily divided into the following categories:

1. The estate workers who constitute the bulk of the Malaysian Indian population;
2. The urban low-income production workers who constitute a significant part of the Malaysian Indian population; and
3. The professional and management class that makes up a small and declining minority of the Malaysian Indian population.

The major thrust to overcoming the Malaysian Indian problem therefore should be where the bulk of its population is found, that is, in the rubber and oil palm estates of Malaysia's heartland.

The urban low-income Malaysian Indians too are spread out and are also in relatively less need of assistance, since their incomes are generally higher than that earned by the estate workers. Their standards of living in terms of education, health and environment are also much better than in the estates. So priority should go towards helping the estate workers to alleviate and improve their impoverished circumstances.

However, the prospects of the Malaysian Indians in the urban areas also need serious attention. In some ways they could be more unsettled, having been uprooted from the estates. Many of them lack basic needs such as inadequate good food (through lack of good employment and income), poor shelter (due to the unaffordability of even squatter rentals) and a shortage of other amenities associated with displacement from the estates.

Malaysian Indians find difficulty in getting hawker licenses, taxi and lorry permits, housing and jobs—even if they have some minimum qualifications. Of course, in times of full employment, they have less problems at finding jobs. But now they have to compete with the hardier Indonesian and Bangladeshi workers for even labourer's jobs.

Measures to Improve the Welfare of Indians

Malaysian Indians in small businesses, like their Bumiputera small-business counterparts, lack access to capital, know-how, markets and contracts. At the same time, unlike the Bumiputera businessmen, they do not have the Government infrastructure to support them.

In the interests of National Unity, it is therefore vital that urban low-income Malaysian Indians be given some priority in the allocation of licenses, permits, housing, contracts and even job quotas. This is necessary to ensure their active participation in the mainstream of economic development. This will be in keeping with the original spirit of the NEP which was to assist *all* the poor, regardless of race.

Estates

In the estates, measures to improve the welfare and prospects of the estate workers should be enhanced. There are, of course, limits as to what estate owners can do to improve the welfare of the existing estate workers. It's also difficult and costly to raise their productivity, education, values and attitudes. However, their environment and quality of life can be improved by looking into three important areas of human welfare, i.e. housing, health and environment.

1. **Housing.** The Workers' Minimum Standards of Housing and Amenities legislation provides for reasonable housing. The Malaysian Indian Congress (MIC) had been given the portfolio of Deputy Minister of the Ministry of Housing in the past. The opportunity was utilised to some extent to raise the

standards of housing in some estates. However, there is much more that needs to be done to improve the squalid housing found in most estates, where housing has often been described as substandard.

It is thus recommended that the Government should strongly enforce the legislation so as to ensure that estate workers not only live in decent housing but are also provided with basic amenities such as clean water and electricity supply. This is not too much to ask of a government committed to promoting a Caring Society.

2. **Health.** Similarly, there are also guidelines to provide for good health care in estate clinics and hospitals. But these provisions have not been fully implemented despite having had an MIC Deputy Minister of Health in the Government at one time. The indicators for infant mortality, life expectancy, malnutrition and the general level of health are about the lowest and most unfavourable for estate workers, as compared to other ethnic groups in the country.

It is thus recommended that the Government ensure that the estate hospitals and clinics are properly staffed and serviced, so that not only Malaysian Indians but all estate workers, regardless of race, can have equal access to proper medical and health-care services.

3. **Environment.** The estate workers cannot be brought into the Malaysian mainstream of development without being exposed to the mass media (such as television, radio, newspapers), the amenities of modern living and especially clean and pleasing environments.

It is recommended that the Government require, through legislation if necessary, that basic minimum environmental standards be introduced and maintained in all estates, regardless of whether they are in Malay, Chinese or Indian areas. A better learning and physical environment will promote higher values and greater hope.

Malaysian Indians' Share of the Corporate Sector

The Malaysian Indians' share of the corporate sector has remained relatively stagnant over the last 25 years, since the New Economic Policy was introduced in 1970. It grew from about 0.8 per cent to only about 1.0 per cent at present. It is not likely to expand at a faster rate in the foreseeable future. This is mainly because:

1. The savings rate in the Malaysian Indian community is low due to their generally low incomes. Hence their limitations to invest in equity and the corporate sector.
2. The Government's privatisation programmes have not provided much opportunity for Malaysian Indians to accumulate equity in the corporate sector or even to get directly involved in privatisation like the Bumiputeras and Chinese. Only a handful of Indians have gained from privatisation.
3. There is no mechanism like the Amanah Saham Nasional and the Permodalan Nasional Berhad to help Malaysian Indians participate in the corporate sector. The Indian-based company, MAIKA, is the closest entity there is, but its record has been far from impressive. The Indians should thus take full advantage of the new Amanah Saham Wawasan 2020.

The 10 per cent equity share of the corporate sector for the Indians is therefore a mere target, which will not be attainable—unless the Government deliberately adopts policies to assist Malaysian Indians to have a fairer share and stake in the Malaysian corporate sector. It would be highly salutary if the Government could be persuaded, in the spirit of National Unity, to introduce a package of specific measures to deliberately enable Malaysian Indians to obtain a bigger stake in the corporate sector.

It is thus recommended that similar schemes like the ASN and PNB could be established for the Malaysian Indians—provided that the Government adopts policies to provide them with new equity shares and greater participation in privatisation. Unless there is Government assistance, it is unlikely that this proposal will be successful. It is also less likely that any new scheme to help the Indians will be adequately supported by the Malaysian Indians since they have been disappointed by similar initiatives in the past.

Human Resource Development

There are serious limitations as to what can be done to alleviate poverty and improve the well-being of Malaysian Indian adults who are currently employed. It is difficult to find the resources to train, educate, rehabilitate and relocate them, especially from the estates to the manufacturing and service sectors in the urban areas.

The solution to the Malaysian Indian problem therefore will be found in helping the Malaysian Indian children, especially those of schoolgoing age who are living in the estates. If the right policy decisions are taken soon, then in 5-10 years' time, we will be able to see positive results that will save the Malaysian Indian children from the quagmire of misery and hopelessness in the estates and slums and allow them to develop and contribute to Malaysia's prosperity. Otherwise, they will remain the weak link in the Malaysian economy.

Tamil Schools

The question is whether the leaders of the Malaysian Indian community are willing to phase out the present inefficient Tamil schools system to the more progressive and beneficial Government's National School System? It is well known that the Tamil schools have about the lowest performance and highest dropout rates compared to the Bumiputeras and Malaysian Chinese students in national or national-type Chinese schools. This is because the Tamil schools and the educational facilities in the estates are woefully inadequate. Furthermore, a high proportion of the teaching staff are untrained and mostly uncommitted. According to the *The Second Round: Vision 2020 and Malaysian Indians*, a publication by the MIC, "Some 90 per cent of the schools lacked trained teachers and proper facilities. The buildings were old and the sanitation poor. There were no playing fields and amenities for health. The schools had been provided not with any real wish to educate the children, but to stop workers from leaving [the estates]." It is no wonder Indian youth constitute the highest proportion of drug addicts and criminals in Malaysia.

How can the products of such schools, with deplorable facilities and unqualified teachers, produce good results and contribute to National Unity? Neglected, these students may grow up frustrated, bitter, reactionary, alienated, ill-educated and even "anti-national".

It is therefore in the interest of stronger National Unity that Malaysian Indian children should be given a better deal by both the MIC and the authorities who formulate and implement education policies.

Despite the generally bad conditions, there are many children from the estate Tamil schools who perform rather well. But most of them are neglected, as a large pool of wasted talent and underdeveloped human resources. Malaysia can least afford this wastage—whether they are Malay, Chinese or Indian.

The ideal solution for Tamil schools then would be for the Government to take over the Tamil Schools and at the same time maintain their present character with Tamil as a medium of instruction and Bahasa Malaysia as an equally strong language. This would mean that Government funds will have to be allocated to improve the infrastructure of the schools and the standard of teaching—and why not, in the interests of national unity.

The Tamil Schools should be gradually phased out over a specified time frame of about ten years and be converted into Bantuan Penuh Tamil Schools with more time for Bahasa Malaysia. This means that the government will have to provide funds to buy over the land sites of the schools at concessionary rates, preferably from the estate owners. I believe the government could also persuade the larger estates to even surrender the small plots of estate land as a contribution to nation-building. After making so much profit through the years, surely the larger estates can make this small contribution to Indian labour and to National Unity.

Needless to say, this is a sensitive subject and therefore has to be examined with great care and caution. But it has to be done, if we are serious about promoting the welfare of Malaysian Indian children, to enhance National Unity and overall national economic welfare.

Implementing the New Tamil School Policy
The following measures can be considered in implementing a new Tamil School Policy.

1. The Tamil Schools that are on private estate lands could be converted to Bantuan Penuh Schools. The Government could persuade private estates to donate the school sites for educational purposes. However, where private estates are reluctant to donate, then the Government and the MIC could raise the necessary funds to buy these school sites. Since these school sites are in the rural areas and are not large pieces (merely 2-3 acres each), these pieces of land are relatively inexpensive. It is recommended that a Land Bank for estate schools should therefore be established for this purpose.

2. The process of consolidating Tamil schools must be accelerated. Then the bigger schools which will be more efficiently run due to economies of scale could be converted to Sekolah Bantuan Penuh.

3. Furthermore, the Government could provide school-bus services for Malaysian Indian and other rural schoolchildren to travel to the consolidated schools in the rural areas, where transport services are unavailable or unsatisfactory.

4. Tamil school teachers who are untrained could be required to undergo special training to upgrade their educational standards and teaching techniques. This could also increase their career prospects. They need not then fear the loss of employment or any decline in their career advancement.

5. As a prerequisite for these proposals to be accepted by the Malaysian Indian community, it is essential that all National Schools provide Pupils' Own Language (POL) classes in Tamil, as a compulsory subject. This would encourage Malay-

sian Indian parents to send their children to national schools, where these children could get a far better education and at the same time learn their mother tongue in a more professional environment.

This positive approach will prevent Malaysian Indian parents from feeling a sense of deprivation and a loss of cultural identity, for otherwise they would be dissuaded from sending their children to national schools. The Government should not just make this offer, but should ensure the proper and effective implementation of this Pupils' Own Language Programme. Otherwise, polarisation in education will continue and contribute little to National Unity.

Conclusion

This chapter examines the Malaysian Indian perspective of National Unity in Malaysia. Regrettably, it is not possible to conclude that there is much interest or belief in National Unity from the Malaysian Indian point of view—except for the educated minority and the well-to-do amongst them.

The majority of Malaysian Indians are in the lower income and poverty groups. Most of them are in the estates where they have been neglected, and isolated from the mainstream of economic growth and modernisation since colonial times, when they came to Malaysia as indentured labour. The alienation that most low-income Malaysian Indians feel has been brought about by the low priority given to them to enhance their welfare. This has been further compounded by the Malaysian Indian leadership's greater concern with their own political and party problems, infighting, survival and individual advancement.

National Unity therefore has been weakened by the relative neglect of the estate workers. National Unity will continue to be eroded if the welfare of the Malaysian Indians is indifferently treated. There must be a new realisation and a new direction towards achieving greater National Unity through enhancing the opportunities and commitment of the Malaysian Indian estate and urban workers to National Unity.

But how can this be achieved? I have outlined several recommendations but the major solution to this Malaysian Indian problem will be found in gradually raising the standards of education of the estate Tamil schools, through converting them to Sekolah Bantuan Penuh and then perhaps to National Schools, within a time frame of within 10 years.

To maintain the *status quo* will be counter productive or inimical and may even provide a convenient way to prolong or gloss over the Malaysian Indian problem. Therefore, in the interests of enhancing National Unity and the achievement of the noble objectives of Dr Mahathir Mohamad's Vision 2020, we have to embark on a concrete programme to revamp the Tamil schools system as soon as possible. Otherwise we would perpetuate the "Green Ghettos" in Malaysia's plantation sector.

The Government, the MIC, Malaysian Indian leadership and parents must act with urgency to help solve the Malaysian Indian problem in the interests of National Unity. Otherwise, the future of the low-income Indians is indeed bleak.

There are only two leaders in Malaysia whose decisions can solve the Malaysian Indian problem. One is our outstanding Prime Minister Dr Mahathir Mohamad and the other is the president of MIC, Dato' Seri Samy Vellu. His predominant position in the MIC would make it easier for him to positively influence the Malaysian Indian community to make the necessary decisions for their integration into the Malaysian mainstream, while still retaining their cultural identity, within the context of National Unity. The sooner this is done the better. Otherwise, the Malaysian Indian community will not be able to contribute effectively to Vision 2020.

PART FIVE
INTERNATIONAL ECONOMIC RELATIONS

22.

DEALING WITH
THE UNITED STATES
AND EUROPE

IN the beginning of this book, the strengths and weaknesses of the Malaysian economy were outlined. It was argued that the economy will continue to perform well, but we will have to take firmer measures to overcome emerging economic problems, especially those emanating from the United States and Europe.

Opportunities

Now, I would like to dwell on some of our opportunities and challenges in the next couple of years. Let's take the international scene and start with our opportunities. There is no doubt that we are witnessing worldwide transformation in economic thought, planning and policies. Historically, it is unprecedented that so many governments and countries have rejected socialist, centralised and government economic intervention. They have been turning to the open and free market capitalistic system, albeit with some modifications to suit each country's culture.

Today, it is becoming more and more the world of the businessman—not the bureaucrat or even the politician. It's the private sector that is expected to lead economic and business transformation and progress. The private sector, with political stability and government backing, is expected to deliver a better standard and quality of life to the public, through competition, business success and prosperity. The world is increasingly becoming a huge global village, with growing emphasis on economic progress, not political ideology. Malaysia's economic opportunities are therefore very attractive.

Asia-Europe Meeting

Take the recent successful conclusion of the Asia-Europe Meeting (ASEM) in Bangkok in February 1996. It was unthinkable just a few years ago. Today, the opportunities for trade, investment and the transfer of technology are immense. The ASEM meeting agreed on many concrete projects for closer economic co-operation between East Asia and Europe. It proposed the establishment of an educational foundation, an environmental technology centre, an investment promotion plan, an Asia-Europe business forum, an ASEM university programme and the development of a railway system stretching from Singapore to China or even Europe. Surely all these provide great incentives for developing stronger economic and trade links within East Asia and with Europe. These great opportunities are also big challenges.

Challenges

For instance, Malaysia will be co-ordinating the railway project. I hope we will take on this challenge to expand investment opportunities abroad. There is no point in Prime Minister Dato Seri Dr Mahathir Mohamad securing the privilege of co-ordinating this huge railway project if our businessmen are not enterprising enough to seize the opportunities for construction, engineering, manufacture of rolling stock and the associated signalling equipment. It will be a real pity if other countries benefit much more than us from this vast project.

A special Malaysian Task Force comprising the government and the private sector could be set up to get our businessmen fully involved in all stages of the planning and implementation of this project. We need to ensure that Malaysia gets a fair share of this huge investment in railways and other massive regional projects like those in the Mekong Basin in Cambodia. Otherwise, we will end up laying the groundwork, while others seize the opportunities.

Indeed, the ASEM was more successful than anticipated. The earlier concerns that the Europeans would raise issues related to the "social clauses" pertaining to human rights, labour rights, etc. were in retrospect, unfounded. Perhaps the Europeans had planned to raise these issues but withdrew them in a subtle and diplomatic move to forestall our strong reaction. That was clever as the ASEM might have otherwise failed even before it could take off.

But the Europeans are smart. After all, they colonised much of Asia and Africa and they understand the timing of their strategy. Why should they raise social issues that would detract them from their aim to increase beneficial business with fast growing Asia.

The Americans, however, are different. They lack the colonial experience and exploitation of the past. They are more concerned with domination and their own narrow self-interests, and tend to act like the bull in the china shop. They lack maturity, style and subtlety.

The US Role in APEC
The diplomatic skills of the Europeans are in sharp contrast to the conduct of the performance of the Americans in APEC. The United States insisted on time frames and targets for members to cut their own import duties. They did not consider seriously the huge problems developing Asian countries would face by drastically reducing or eliminating protective import duties and penetrating their markets.

The United States did not give due consideration to the fact that some Asian countries are still so underdeveloped compared to the vastly rich United States, and that Asian countries are so different in their various stages of socio-economic development. Perhaps they know, but do not care. Why should they? They are big and so they think they can bully others—and they do or try to do so all the time.

The United States was neither pragmatic nor diplomatic. Neither were they caring. This is the difference between the United States and Europe. This new Asian alliance with Europe will now enable Asia to balance the United States against Europe in helping to create a more even playing field and fair competition in trade and investment. All these developments emphasise the need for East Asia to give higher priority to further developing its ties with Europe. Otherwise, Asia will be dominated by the United States. This could be disastrous not only in the economic but political areas. We do not need nor desire another kind of colonialism or economic imperialism. But it seems to be coming back through the World Trade Organisation and APEC!

The challenge then is for the United States to hopefully learn to live with East Asia as an equal partner. Now that we have Europe to fall back on, this challenge should be easier to deal with. The strength of our economic relations in APEC will have to depend more on a project rather than a policy approach. This strategy will enhance the prospects for genuine partnership with both the European and the US trading blocs.

Since Malaysia will be chairing the APEC meeting in 1998, we should start work now to level out the playing fields of trade and investment in the APEC region, so that East Asia—and not just the United States and Japan—can benefit from liberalisation in the APEC. We should all benefit as equitably as possible. Otherwise, APEC will fail .

From economics, we move to human rights. Here, the US government has put its foot in again. There is much to be admired in the United States; so, I cannot understand why the United States should continue to bumble along in its international relations.

Human Rights
The US government's 20th Annual Report on Human Rights has drawn criticism and scorn from the non-Western world. China has led in the protests against the report which its scholar Ren Yanshi describes as "sheer fabrication and distortion". Dr Mahathir Mohamad has also severely criticised the United States and asked them to examine their own backyard. But they hardly do as they tend to look at others more closely.

Indeed those who live in glass houses should not throw stones. No country in the world is perfect. The United States itself has glaring examples of serious violations of human rights throughout its history. Now Tan Sri Musa Hitam has announced that the United States itself has been declared a violator of human rights by the United Nations Commission on Human Rights. This is indeed the height of irony. The whole credibility of the US policies and preaching can now be called to question. Malaysia, like many other countries, seeks to improve its standard of living, quality of life and human welfare. But all this cannot be achieved without stronger societal discipline and some sacrifice of absolute individual human freedom. However, we should strive to strike a fair and reasonable compromise between concern for the individual and that of the society as a whole. In our Asian cultures, the community and society come first and the individual's self-interest comes last.

The United States should understand the problems of the Third World, as the United States has also had the experience of moving through the many stages of underdevelopment to the powerful economy the United States is today. But instead, by her actions, the US gives the impression that she is not prepared to see dynamic Third World countries advance in economic growth, industrialisation and modernisation.

The United States must review its policies towards the Third World or risk being regarded as an economic bully trying to use all manner of devious methods to keep developing countries economically depressed so that the United States can dominate them.

The Third World could help the United States understand that we too know what is good for us. For instance, US Ambassador to Malaysia John Mallot's recent statement that the EAEC proposal should be left to the people of the region to decide is great. But it begs the question as to whether the United States will allow some of its allies in East Asia to decide independently without any interference or coercion from the United States. Will the United States encourage democracy or exercise dominance? That would be the challenge for the United States to face.

23.

LESSONS LEARNT AT
OSAKA'S APEC MEETING

HISTORY will show that Malaysia actually saved the Asia-Pacific Economic Co-operation (APEC) meeting in Osaka in November 1995 from a breakdown and breakup. The credit for this salvation should go to Prime Minister Dato Seri Dr Mahathir Mohamad and Trade and Industry Minister Dato' Seri Rafidah Aziz and their dedicated civil servants. They battled hard to be different and to lead APEC back on track and towards a satisfactory agenda for action.

Problem
What was the problem in Osaka? The trouble started at the APEC meeting in Bogor, Indonesia. There, the heads of government agreed to a common resolve to set targets for free and open trade and investment by the year 2020: the developing economies to attain the target by 2020 and the industrial economies by 2010. How can there be a difference of only ten years for structural socio-economic adjustments of such huge magnitude?

How can any leader commit himself to set definite targets to open national markets, regardless of one's own national interests? Furthermore, these commitments cannot be rigid nor legal. Neither can they be binding on any country. It is neither realistic nor fair to the Asian countries, and one asks whether there is duress or just plain agreement only in principle and not in practice?

Nevertheless, all the eighteen economies in APEC agreed to the Bogor Declaration. Malaysia alone dared to be different and expressed its opposition to the fixed time frame for liberalisation. We considered it unreasonable as it would be unfair to force countries to conform to rigid targets that could be against their own national interests and even survival. But the United States does not understand this great dilemma. Perhaps it does, but it would like to dominate the weaker economies. Could this APEC onslaught be a grand economic design on the part of the United States to dominate Asia? We will have to watch what the United States do very carefully.

Opposition
At the following APEC meeting in Osaka, Japan, at least four major members expressed opposition to liberalising trade and investment in their agricultural sectors. How could China, Japan, South Korea and Taiwan whose populations have rice as their staple food allow their rice production and trade to be completely opened to stiff competition from abroad. The United States, Canada, Australia and New Zealand are far more efficient food producers. What then would happen to the livelihood of the millions of rice farmers in these Asian countries? That is why the Asian countries protested, while the non-Asian APEC members pushed their case for comprehensive liberalisation, regardless of the internal socio-economic disruption it could cause. Do the Caucasian countries in the APEC want instability in Asia. They have to clarify their strategies, otherwise deep-seated suspicions will rise to the surface.

Truth and reality came to life in Osaka. Malaysia's stand in Bogor was vindicated. The division was so severe that, if the United States and its non-Asian allies had dug in and resisted the Asian views, APEC's future could have been jeopardised. APEC's future could still be in danger.

Malaysia's Stand
This is where Malaysia's insistence on the inclusion of the phrase "nonbinding" won the day. The Bogor Declaration and the Osaka Declaration are now to be regarded as only declarations of intent and not binding agreements. Legally or morally, national priorities will predominate

now. Countries that can meet the indicative targets will do so. Those that cannot, for whatever reasons, need not, if it is not in their national interests to do so. They have to decide on their targets and timing, and not be imposed upon by the rich and powerful countries.

Indeed, that is how it should have been in Bogor. APEC should follow the example of Asean where no country can take advantage of another. Even Indonesia, which is by far the largest country in Asean, does not impose its will on smaller members. It is not the Asian or Asean way. The West needs to understand and appreciate our values. They will be able to benefit from our longer history and wisdom.

The United States' Stance

This is where the United States was found lacking. Because of its dominant role in international affairs and due to its economic and military dominance, the United States tends to want to dominate wherever and whenever it can. It becomes insensitive and arrogant as is the way with most rich and powerful nations and individuals. They talk overbearingly of "great nations keeping their commitments" as if they have kept all their promises and commitments in the past, except when its own vital interests are involved. The United States should not pretend to be altruistic when it has no intention of being so. It should not preach altruism when it practices economic aggression, and even economic imperialism when it wants to compete on uneven playing fields, with strong and weak players.

Australia and New Zealand's Mistake

Unfortunately too, Australia, which initiated the formation of APEC, lost a golden opportunity in Osaka. It could have played Malaysia's role in Osaka. As an aspiring Asian nation, it should have taken the initiative to show better understanding of Asian needs and sensitivities. Instead, it chose again to toe the US line, and fought for its own narrow agricultural interests. It was a mistake for both Australia and New Zealand in their strategy in dealing with Asia. What a pity! There is a need for them to rectify their mistake of forsaking Asia where they belong.

How can Australia and even New Zealand claim a role in Asia when they think and act in ways contrary to the Asian way. They cannot have their hearts in the United Kingdom and the United States and try to keep their minds in Asia. They have to show by thought, word and deed than their souls are in Asia. They should heed the lesson of Osaka. Perhaps the Australian Asian Institute, which aims to promote better Australian-Asian relations, will be better able to achieve its objectives.

Lessons from Osaka

What are the lessons that can be learnt from the Osaka meeting?

First, it pays to be truthful, even if we are called mavericks or other names. In the end, truth will prevail as it did in Osaka. Our Asian compatriots will need to be more western in their style, in dealing with the westerners. We need to be more open—and blunt, if we have to. Otherwise we will be misunderstood or even taken for granted.

Second, because of Malaysia's economic independence and non-reliance on foreign aid, it can afford to be outspoken. It is a great asset to be able to speak up for so many others who cannot, because of their dependence on, or fear of, the rich and powerful countries.

Third, although we are a small country, we have learnt that we can still resist the coercion and domineering attitudes of the bigger and more powerful nations. We should, therefore, carry on firmly but in our polite way.

Fourth, we need not follow consensus but we can lead in building consensus. This came out clearly in Bogor. Malaysia did not follow consensus blindly, but instead worked hard to persuade others to resist dominance, because our leaders had the courage of their conviction.

Fifth, we should never give up against heavy odds, even at the international level. If Malaysia did not persist at Bogor and then at Osaka, we would have been overwhelmed by the narrow self-interests of the United States and its allies in APEC. Our leaders' persistence enabled the silent majority within APEC to rally round quietly to support the voluntary 'non-binding' philosophy enunciated by Malaysia in the Osaka Action

Agenda. That is to say that we need not be legally or morally bound by intentions of policy changes.

Lessons for the Caucasians in APEC

What are the lessons for the United States and its Caucasian supporters (Australia and New Zealand) in APEC?

First, they should not try to dominate us in Asia nor try to dominate the Asian economies. It is easier to do so in Europe where there are many strong cultural and ethnic bonds and a great deal of gratitude to the United States for past services, especially during the world wars. Even Japan can be dominated by the United States.

Second, they should try to be more sensitive to Asian cultures and thinking in economic and political diplomacy. The Asian "Dragons" and "Tigers" and the developing countries are diverse. Nevertheless, they are determined not to be dominated by alien prescription for their own socio-economic development and management strategies. The Caucasians should work together with us rather than talk down to us. Do not try to lead Asians by their noses, especially when it is for your own benefit.

Third, please keep your own house in order first, before telling others what is good for their economies. After all, poor economic performances, untenable budget and balance of payments deficits, and the inability to pay civil servants, are not good examples to emulate. US President Bill Clinton should give priority to the US budget problems over trying to promote free trade in APEC. Similarly, it is only fair that APEC members be allowed to liberalise flexibly according to their own national interests. Charity begins at home.

Fourth, might is not always right. Also, what is sauce for the goose may not be good for the gander. Listen more and shape your ideas and policies to accommodate all views and not sectarian and vested interests only. That is the genius of *musyawarah and muafakat*, which stands for genuine "consultation and consensus". These are Asean and even good universal values that can be followed for mutual benefit.

APEC's Future

What of the future of APEC? If APEC members are prepared to learn from their mistakes and experiences, then APEC will flourish. If not, it will fade away, or fizzle out over the medium term.

It is acknowledged that the potential of APEC is great. Many more countries in the Pacific Rim can be admitted into it. Already, the 18 members alone produce about 40 per cent of the world's exports and imports. Their combined gross national product is a whopping US$13 trillion (RM33.15 trillion). This is mind boggling. Increased trade and investment in this fast-growing Asia-Pacific region will bring enormous wealth and far higher standards of living and quality of life for the many millions in this region. But it has to come gradually. More haste means less progress.

APEC Ministerial Meeting in Malaysia in 1998

We look forward to APEC's further progress and success. The next Ministerial Meeting in Manila will be followed by the 10th Ministerial Meeting in Kuala Lumpur in 1998. At these annual Ministerial conferences, the progress of trade liberalisation made by member countries will be reviewed. Those members whose progress is slow will presumably be encouraged to do more.

However, no punitive action can be taken against those countries that do not move as fast as some others. They will themselves suffer from the disadvantages of closed markets, and will have to adjust and liberalise according to their own pace and in accordance with their national priorities. They must not be bulldozed or bullied into accepting standards imposed by the powerful over the weak.

Finally, we can be proud of what Malaysia has achieved at the Osaka meeting. The rich and powerful nations would have learnt never to take Malaysia for granted and that Asia has its own identity and aspirations which are realistic and must be respected. Don't push Asia around. It could react like the Japanese did in 1940! The West should learn lessons from history with wisdom and not arrogance which could blind them to reality and equity.

East Asia Economic Caucus

Now that APEC had been put on track, we need to step up Asean's efforts to strengthen APEC through the formation of the East Asia Economic Caucus (EAEC). However, it would appear that the EAEC has in reality already taken off without fanfare. The meeting of the seven Asean countries plus the three Asian giants, i.e. China, Japan and South Korea, will actually constitute what could be the basis for EAEC membership. The meeting of the Asean plus Three to prepare for the Asia-Europe Meeting (ASEM) in February 1996 in Thailand provided the impetus for the further development of APEC. The EAEC can strengthen APEC rather than weaken it, contrary to the logic of some countries.

The action agenda was set realistically in Osaka. Now we can move more purposefully and confidently. Since the agenda is fair and reasonable, let us now go for the action, to make APEC really work for the greater prosperity of the nations of the Pacific Rim and those of the EAEC. There must be a holistic approach. The eastern Pacific Rim should not be allowed to dominate the western Pacific Rim.

There is no doubt in my mind that the United States and other Caucasian countries in the APEC will have to recognise the logic and reality of EAEC within APEC. In fact, the United States in particular, by its sheer domineering stance, will awaken the fears and suspicions of Asians against the United States. They will be forced to consult and collaborate amongst one another to face the US threat to the Asian aspiration to live and flourish in harmony amongst themselves, without interference or dominance from the North and the West via the United States within APEC.

24.

THE WORLD TRADE
ORGANISATION AND
THE THIRD WORLD

MOST Malaysians know so little about the World Trade Organisation (WTO). Yet this new organisation will have a major impact on all of Malaysia's economic and human welfare prospects. The impact will be felt soon and definitely in the next few years.

The WTO was established on January 1, 1995. It succeeded the General Agreement on Tariffs and Trade (GATT) after many years of tough discussions under what is known as the Uruguay Round of negotiations. Total membership of WTO is now about 120 countries which account for about 90 per cent of total world trade.

The GATT dealt with trade in goods like rubber, tin, palm oil and manufactures, but the WTO covers a much wider field. It includes trade in Services like banking, insurance, intellectual property rights, dumping of goods and numerous barriers to trade.

The WTO is now monitoring the world's trade practices like a watchdog and will supervise all future trade reviews, disputes and negotiations. It will affect our economic growth, our incomes and our employment. Indeed it may well be the most powerful international organisation. It could be even more important than the United Nations itself in terms of directly affecting our individual lives. This is because the WTO, unlike the United Nations, will have teeth to "punish" countries that violate its principles. It will also have the "power" to dominate the poorer, smaller and weaker countries.

The WTO can become the new weapon to "exploit" the Third World and to reintroduce neo-economic colonialism if developing countries are not careful. The industrial countries in the North are already preparing to introduce all kinds of ways and means to continue to dominate world trade and investment, through their strong negotiating power in the WTO.

Malaysia and other countries in the Third World must also prepare for the oncoming fight, otherwise we will lose even before it starts. Dato' Seri Rafidah Aziz has taken the initiatives, but are we all following up adequately?

I do not think the business sector is fully aware of the serious implications nor is it ready to take on the new challenges of the WTO. But it is the business sector that ironically will suffer the most.

The first WTO Ministerial Meeting was held in December 1996 in Singapore. Were we prepared? This meeting set the stage for a continuing conflict with the rich industrial countries. They went all out to fight the poor and emerging developing countries, preventing them from getting a bigger share of world trade, investment and wealth.

WTO's New Issues
To continue dominating the South, rich countries want to introduce "new issues" into the WTO negotiations such as the following:

First, by introducing discriminatory trade measures against countries which, in their view, do not adequately protect the environment. Now this could be aimed at countries like Malaysia as an excuse to protect the trade of the rich countries. The industrial countries pollute the environment with wasteful utilisation of energy and emission of fumes. However, they insist that we preserve our forests to enable them to continue to pollute the atmosphere even more, in order to safeguard their high standards of living.

The rich countries on the other hand will flagrantly ignore the provisions of Article XX of the WTO that allows members to undertake measures necessary to protect human life. They will expect us to be indifferent to eradicating poverty in the Third World, if it means some clearing of our forests for economic development. But the poor could not survive as they have to depend on employment in wood-based industries.

Similarly, child labour in some countries could provide that vital income for some families. We should not be expected to pay for the pollution and the past sins of environmental exploitation by the industrial countries, But the new rules they want to introduce in the WTO could just do that—to make us pay for their continued prosperity and progress at our expense! We must be very careful because they are trying to change the "rules of the game" to suit themselves!

Second, the rich countries have been raising Competition Issues which were further pursued at the WTO meeting in Singapore. These issues relate to: preventing the promotion of our pioneer industries, which we protect with tax incentives; and linking labour standards with trade. Thus a country with labour standards unacceptable to industrial countries could be barred from exporting to the industrial countries. For instance, if the rich countries insist on employment insurance and public welfare schemes that have practically ruined their own economies, the Third World countries will have to adopt similar unproductive policies. Can you imagine the havoc it will cause, especially to highly populated countries like China, India and Indonesia, if they have to give unemployment insurance and public welfare assistance to their people? Their economies will be seriously undermined. But that may be just what some industrial countries want. This will enable them to continue to dominate the world. This is the so-called "social clause" weapon, which we in the Third World will have to shoot down, before it explodes on us!

But the worst weapon in this forthcoming "WTO War" relates to the new Multilateral Investment Agreement.

A fascinating comment by Martin Khor of the Third World Network in Penang on the Proposed Foreign Investment Treaty indicates how destructive this new proposal could become. The rich countries are proposing that Foreign Direct Investment should have free access to developing countries. They are pushing for National Treatment for foreign investors. This means that developing countries have to treat foreign investors like their own national investors for purposes of tax and other incentives.

This simply means that the new rules proposed by the rich countries will allow them to come to Malaysia uninvited, and buy over 100 per cent of the equity share of any company at a mutually agreed price. If government policies do not allow this transaction for political and strategic reasons, then the WTO could take punitive action against the host country. If this rule is adopted by the WTO, then no country can protect its national sovereignty in trade and investment policies. We might as well become colonies once again!

In Malaysia, there is already some pressure to change the investment rules to allow foreigners the right to tender for Malaysian Government contracts and Privatisation Schemes and to allow foreign professionals to move freely in and out of our country. Our professionals like accountants, doctors, lawyers and engineers could be adversely affected. All this could undermine our national interests, especially since Malaysia is still a developing country.

All Malaysians should therefore rally round the Government to strongly resist the attempts by the rich countries to change the rules of the WTO to suit their own interests. We must prepare now to win the battles looming within the WTO or lose the trade war and decline.

I attended the Third World Network Conference in Geneva on 10-11 September 1996 organised by its leader Martin Khor of Penang. I was struck by the state of unpreparedness on the part of the Third World ambassadors and their lack of adequate consultation and co-ordination, to face the onslaught from the North in Singapore at the 1st World Trade Conference in December 1996.

Unless we in the Third World co-operate and put up a unified resistance, the West will divide and rule and get their way to dominate us under a new world order of economic imperialism once again.

Is is hoped that the Third World countries will gain enough support and a unity of purpose to deny some of the West and the northern industrial countries their devious designs to dominate the developing countries of the South through the WTO.

Conclusion

The battle will not end in Singapore. The conflict will carry on. The developing countries will have to continue their fight to preserve and protect their political and economic independence, national sovereignty and self-respect.

The lesson we should learn from the WTO Ministerial Meeting in Singapore in December 1996 is that, developing countries must strengthen their fraternity and co-operation. The North or the developed countries will continue to try to dominate the South or the developing countries. The United States will lead the North. The developing countries will have to choose their own leaders to ensure that they are not marginalised in the new 21st century as well.

Instead, the developing countries must aim for fully developed nation status where all its citizens will enjoy the blessings of God's great global gifts on an equitable basis and with human dignity.

INDEX

Abdul Rahman, Tunku, 6, 82, 123
Abdul Razak Hussein, Tun, 7, 82, 123, 147
Abu Bakar Jaafar, Dato' Dr, 139
Abu Bakar Sulaiman, Tan Sri Dr, 62
ADB, *see* Asian Development Bank
Afta, *see* Asean Free Trade Area
Ahmad Mohd Don, Dato, 42
Ahmad Sarji Abdul Hamid, Tan Sri, 61, 110
Amanah Ikhtiar Malaysia, 31, 43
Amanah Saham Nasional, 135, 163
Amanah Saham Wawasan 2020, 135, 163
Anwar Ibrahim, Dato' Seri, 27, 42, 54, 64, 146
APEC, *see* Asia-Pacific Economic Co-operation
Asean Free Trade Area, 16
ASEM, *see* Asia-Europe Meeting
Asia-Europe Meeting, 172-173, 183
Asia-Pacific Economic Co-operation, 76-77, 173-174, 177-183
Asian Development Bank, 48-49
ASN, *see* Amanah Saham Nasional
Australian Asian Institute, 180

Balance of payments, 22, 28-29, 41, 45
Bank Bumiputera Malaysia, 119
Bank Negara Malaysia, 10, 41-42, 81
Bank Simpanan Nasional, 119
Barisan Nasional, 39, 43, 66, 122, 143
BCIC, *see* Bumiputera Commercial and Industrial Community
BNM, *see* Bank Negara Malaysia
Bogor Declaration, 178
Brudtland Commission, 137
Bumiputera Commercial and Industrial Community, 73, 82
Business Conditions Survey, 55

Caring Society, 30, 119, 133, 148, 162
Clarke, Kenneth, 64
Client's Charter, 61
Clinton, Bill, 181
Code of Ethics for Ministers, 144
Congress of Unions of Employees in the Public and Civil Services, 34, 103, 105
Constitution, Malaysian, 155

Consumer Price Index, 21, 27-28, 37, 40, 68, 116
Consumer Price Index for Non-Controlled Items, 68
Consumer Price Index Lower Income Group, 37
Corruption, 35, 129-135
CPI LIG, see Consumer Price Index Lower Income Group
CPI, see Consumer Price Index
CPINCI, see Consumer Price Index for Non-Controlled Items
Cuepacs, see Congress of Unions of Employees in the Public and Civil Services

Daim Zainuddin, Tun, 7
Department of Environment, 63, 138, 140-141
Department of Irrigation and Drainage, 140-141
DID, see Department of Irrigation and Drainage
DOE, see Department of Environment
Domestic Investment Fund, 73
Domestic Violence Act 1995, 147

EAEC, see East Asia Economic Caucus
East Asia Economic Caucus, 41, 76-77, 175, 183
Economic Planning Unit, 9-10, 42, 50, 81
Emergency, 4
Environmental Watch Group, 141
EPU, see Economic Planning Unit

Fiscal policy, 73
Federation of Malaysian Consumer Associations, 145

Flexi Wage System, 90, 116
FOMCA, see Federation of Malaysian Consumer Associations
Foreign Direct Investment, 187

GATT, see General Agreement on Tariffs and Trade
GDP, see Gross Domestic Product
General Agreement on Tariffs and Trade, 185
Generalised System of Preferences, 56
GNP, see Gross National Product
Gramin Bank Scheme, 43
Gross Domestic Product, 13, 24, 54, 133
Gross National Product, 29, 45
GSP, see Generalised System of Preferences

Hamdan Adnan, 145
Harun Din, Dato', 145
Heritage Foundation, Washington, 71
Housing, 28, 40-41, 64-66, 74, 112, 133, 153, 161-162
  low-cost, 64-66, 74, 117
HRDF, see Human Resource Development Fund
Human Resource Development Fund, 89
Hussein Onn, Tun, 82, 123

IAPG, see Inter Agency Macro Planning Group
ICOR, see Incremental Capital Output Ratio
IMC, see Institute of Management Consultants
IMF, see International Monetary Fund

Immigration Department, 134
Income distribution, 36
Income per capita, 3
Incremental Capital Output Ratio, 87, 116
Index of Economic Freedom, 71
Inflation, 3, 21-22, 25, 27, 29, 33-38, 40, 42, 53, 56-57, 92, 133, 146
Inland Revenue Department, 118
Institute of Management Consultants, 49-50
Inter Agency Macro Planning Group, 81
International Monetary Fund, 67, 149-150
IRD, *see* Inland Revenue Department
ISO 9000, 84

Japan-Malaysia Technical Institute, 89

Khor, Martin, 187-188

Langkawi Declaration on Environment, 139
Law, Hieng Ding, 139
Leadership ideals, 121-125
Lee, H.S., Tun, 7
Lim, Ah Lek, Dato', 55, 70
Look East Policy, 41
Lower Certificate of Education, *see* Sijil Rendah Pelajaran

Mahathir Mohamad, Dato Seri Dr, 10, 15, 18, 33, 40, 43, 49, 54, 61, 64, 76, 82, 91, 110, 123, 135, 139, 144, 149, 155, 168, 172, 174, 177
MAIKA, 158, 163

Malayan Banking, 119
Malaysia Airlines, 23
Malaysia Incorporated, 10, 18
Malaysian Administrative and Diplomatic Services, 95, 111
Malaysian Administrative Modernisation and Management Planning Unit, 50
Malaysian Certificate of Education, 158
Malaysian External Trade Development Corporation, 50
Malaysian French Institute, 89
Malaysian Indian Congress, 158, 161-162, 164, 166, 168
Malaysian Institute of Economic Research, 55, 70
Malaysian International Shipping Corporation, 23
Mallot, John, 175
Mampu, *see* Malaysian Administrative Modernisation and Management Planning Unit
Management Buyouts, 93
MATRADE, *see* Malaysian External Trade Development Corporation
MBOs, *see* Management Buyouts
MCE, *see* Malaysian Certificate of Education
MIC, *see* Malaysian Indian Congress
MIER, *see* Malaysian Institute of Economic Research
Ministry of Domestic Trade and Consumer Affairs, 37
Ministry of Health, 63
Ministry of Housing, 161
Ministry of Human Resources, 69
MISC, *see* Malaysian International Shipping Corporation
Mohd Najib Tun Abdul Razak, Dato' Sri, 84, 146

Monetary policy, 25
Money politics, 135
MSC, *see* Multimedia Super
    Corridor
Multilateral Investment Agreement,
    187
Multimedia Super Corridor, 18, 119
Musa Hitam, Tan Sri, 174

National Competitive Policy, 94, 97
National Development Policy, 8,
    17-19, 26, 36, 43, 47, 85, 88, 94,
    97, 132, 134, 155
National Education Policy, 156
National Labour Advisory Council
    on Wage Reform, 69
National Registration Department,
    35, 118
National unity, 33-34, 45, 54, 85,
    94, 113, 152, 154-161, 163,
    165-168
NDP, *see* National Development
    Policy
NEP, *see* New Economic Policy
New Economic Policy, 8, 37, 43, 85,
    132, 155-156, 159-160, 163
New Remuneration Scheme, 106,
    110-111
New Villages, 14
Newly Industrialising Country, 3
Ng, Kam Chiu, 62
NIC, *see* Newly Industrialising
    Country
NRS, *see* New Remuneration
    Scheme

Osaka Declaration, 178-179

PCB, *see* Public Complaints Bureau
Pegawai Tadbiran dan Diplomatik,
    101-103, 111, 113

Penilaian Menengah Rendah, 151
Permodalan Nasional Berhad, 163
PMR, *see* Penilaian Menengah
    Rendah
PNB, *see* Permodalan Nasional
    Berhad
POL, *see* Pupils' Own Language
Pollution, 63, 137-142, 146, 187
Poverty, 3, 13-14, 31, 43, 56, 74, 82,
    85, 149-150, 153, 156, 159, 164,
    167, 186
Poverty line, 56
Privatisation, 11-12, 18, 105, 146,
    163-164, 188
Program Pembangunan Rakyat
    Termiskin, 43
PSD, *see* Public Service Department
PTD, *see* Pegawai Tadbiran dan
    Diplomatik
Public Complaints Bureau, 62, 118
Public Service Department, 102
Pupils' Own Language, 167

R&D, *see* Research and
    Development
Rafidah Aziz, Dato' Seri, 177, 186
Razaleigh Hamzah, Tengku, 7
Red Book, 147
Ren, Yanshi, 174
Research and Development, 84, 90
Rio Earth Summit 1992, 137
Road Transport Department, 35, 63
Royal Customs and Excise
    Department, 134
RTD, *see* Road Transport
    Department
Rukunegara, 155

Saleha Mohd Ali, Dato Paduka, 49
Sambanthan, Tun, 6
Samy Vellu, Dato' Seri, 168

7th Malaysia Plan (1996-2000),
9, 16, 21-22, 25, 31, 59, 65-66,
81-82, 84-85, 87-88
Sijil Rendah Pelajaran, 83
6th Malaysia Plan (1991-1995),
81, 89
Skim Saraan Baru, *see* New
Remuneration Scheme
SRP, *see* Sijil Rendah Pelajaran

Tan, Siew Sin, Tun, 6-7, 45-46
Tenaga Nasional Berhad, 145
TFP, *see* Total Factor Productivity
Third World Network, 187-188
Total Factor Productivity, 82, 87-88
Total Net Factor Productivity, 16
Total Quality Management, 84, 105
TQM, *see* Total Quality
Management
Trade Related Investment Measures,
16
Treasury, 10, 50, 73, 81, 102, 141
TRIMs, *see* Trade Related
Investment Measures

UMNO, *see* United Malay National
Organisation
UNDP Social Index, 152
Unemployment, 151
United Malay National
Organisation, 121, 135
United Nations, 185
United Nations Commission on
Human Rights, 174-175

Vision 2020, 18-19, 39, 43, 45, 54,
61, 81, 94-95, 97, 101, 105-106,
113, 132, 135, 137, 148, 155,
157, 159-160, 168

Water Quality Index, 140
WHO, *see* World Health
Organisation
World Bank, 49, 149-150
World Health Organisation, 140
World Trade Organisation, 16-18,
47, 59, 83, 92, 94, 174, 185-188
WTO, *see* World Trade Organisation

Zero inflation, 27, 33, 37

TAN Sri Dato' Ramon V. Navaratnam is a distinguished former civil servant and corporate personality.

He was an Economist in the Malaysian Treasury for 27 years and rose to become Deputy Secretary-General. During that time he also served as Alternate Director on the Board of Directors of the World Bank in Washington, D.C., and was directly involved in the preparation of the annual national budgets and five-year economic plans. He then became the Secretary-General of the Ministry of Transport in 1986. After his retirement from the civil service in 1989, he was appointed the CEO of Bank Buruh for 5 years, where he raised its profits significantly.

He is now Corporate Adviser to the SungeiWay Group of Companies, Executive Director of Sunway College and Director of the Asian Strategy Leadership Institute (ASLI).